Chicago Public Library
C
P
L
REFERENCE
Form 178 rev. 1-94

The Encyclopedia of
North American Indians

Volume VIII

Ojibwe Literature, Contemporary – Rosebud Reservation

General Editor
D. L. Birchfield

Marshall Cavendish
New York • London • Toronto

Published in 1997 by
Marshall Cavendish Corporation
99 White Plains Road
Tarrytown, NY 10591-9001
U.S.A.

Developed, designed, and produced by Water Buffalo Books, Milwaukee

Project director: Mark J. Sachner
General editor: D. L. Birchfield
Art director: Sabine Beaupré
Photo researcher: Diane Laska
Project editor: Valerie J. Weber

Editors: Elizabeth Kaplan, MaryLee Knowlton, Judith Plumb, Carolyn Kott Washburne

Consulting editors: Donna Beckstrom, Jack D. Forbes, Annette Reed Crum, John Bierhorst

Picture credits: © Archive Photos: 1014, 1021, 1024, 1025, 1048, 1065, 1076 (top), 1082, 1105, 1119, 1140, 1141; © Archive Photos/Popperfoto: 1149; © 1995 Noella Ballenger: Cover; © Steve Bly: 1089, 1123, 1124; © Kit Breen: title, 1086, 1088; © J. Pat Carter/Gamma Liaison: 1016, 1116, 1118; © Corbis-Bettmann: 1037, 1040, 1042, 1055, 1062, 1076 (bottom), 1079, 1117, 1131, 1150; Photo © Addison Doty, Courtesy of Morning Star Gallery: 1035, 1051, 1110, 1122, 1125; © Barry Durand, Odyssey Productions: 1096; © Robert Frerck, Odyssey Productions: 1019; © Walter Frerck, Odyssey Productions: 1095; © Kenneth Gabrielsen/Gamma Liaison: 1115; © Hampton University Archives, Hampton, Virginia: 1023, 1068, 1069; © Kevin O. Mooney, Odyssey Productions: 1101; Collection of Moshe ben-Shimon: 1135; © Tom Myers Photography 1995: 1112; © Leslie M. Newman: 1085, 1087; Courtesy of Louis Owens: 1041; © Reuters/Corbis-Bettmann: 1107; © Renato Rotolo/Gamma Liaison: 1059, 1060, 1074; © Susan Silberberg: 1144, 1145; © Ann Simmons-Myers: 1108; © STOCK MONTAGE, INC.: 1020, 1053, 1057, 1080, 1138, 1139; © Stephen Trimble: 1032, 1033, 1045, 1046, 1047, 1070, 1093, 1094, 1097, 1099, 1109, 1121, 1126, 1137, 1146, 1147; © UPI/Corbis-Bettmann: 1034, 1036, 1043, 1063, 1073, 1098, 1103, 1128; © Diana Walker/Gamma Liaison: 1114; © 1992 S. Kay Young: 1111; © 1989 Jim Yuskavitch: 1029; © 1991 Jim Yuskavitch: 1030, 1084; © 1993 Jim Yuskavitch: 1028

Library of Congress Cataloging-in-Publication Data

The encyclopedia of North American Indians.
p. cm.
Includes bibliographical references and index.
Summary: A comprehensive reference work on the culture and history of Native Americans.
ISBN 0-7614-0235-7 (vol. 8) ISBN 0-7614-0227-6 (lib. bdg.: set)
1. Indians of North America--Encyclopedias, Juvenile.
[1. Indians of North America--Encyclopedias.]
E76.2.E53 1997
970.004'97'003--dc20 96-7700
CIP
AC

Printed and bound in Italy

Title page illustration: Ancient Anasazi pictographs from a site at Canyon de Chelly, Arizona. The Anasazis, considered to be ancestors of various Pueblo peoples in the Southwest, left a legacy that has both historical and artistic value.

Editor's note: Many systems of dating have been used by different cultures throughout history. *The Encyclopedia of North American Indians* uses B.C.E. (Before Common Era) and C.E. (Common Era) instead of B.C. (Before Christ) and A.D. (Anno Domini, "In the Year of the Lord") out of respect for the diversity of the world's peoples.

Contents

the American Indian Literature and Critical Studies Series for the University of Oklahoma Press. His books include *Darkness in Saint Louis Bearheart; Wordarrows: Indians and Whites in the New Fur Trade; Earth Divers: Tribal Narratives on Mixed Descent; Griever: An American Monkey King in China; The Trickster of Liberty: Tribal Heirs to a Wild Baronage; Crossbloods: Bone Courts, Bingo, and other Reports; The Heirs of Columbus; Landfill Meditation: Crossblood Stories;* and *Dead Voices: Natural Agonies in the New World.*

— D. L. Birchfield

SEE ALSO:
North American Indian Prose Award; Ojibwe; Returning the Gift.

OKLAHOMA

A nineteenth-century portrait of an Osage mother and child. Dozens of Indian tribes are still represented in Oklahoma following the removal of eastern tribes to Indian Territory (today's Oklahoma) in the 1800s. The Osages, however, are the only tribe that has a reservation in the state.

Oklahoma became the forty-sixth U.S. state on November 16, 1907. The name *Oklahoma* comes from a Choctaw word for "red man." Of all the U.S. states, Oklahoma has had the most complex relationship with American Indians.

American Indians have lived in the area that is now called Oklahoma for a very long time. Archaeological sites in western Oklahoma reveal that Indians have lived in the area from as long ago as 13,000 B.C.E.

The first Europeans to visit Oklahoma were Spanish conquistador Francisco Vásquez de Coronado and his army, who moved across part of the region in 1541. It was over 150 years later, in 1817, that Auguste Pierre Chouteau established the first European settlement in Oklahoma at Salina. At the time that Chouteau established his town, there were three major tribes who occupied parts of Oklahoma: the Comanches, the Wichitas, and the Kiowas. In addition to dealing with Chouteau and non-Indian settlers, these tribes would soon have much more to confront.

As part of the Indian Removal Act of 1830 and the Indian Trade and Intercourse Act of 1834, Oklahoma, Kansas, Nebraska, South Dakota, and North Dakota were designated as "Indian Territory." Early U.S. explorers of the Great Plains area had called the region "the Great American Desert." Members of the U.S. government truly believed that the area wasn't fit for settlement, and they decided that this region was the perfect place to put Indians from east of the Mississippi. The U.S. government signed treaties with the tribes in Oklahoma that called for those tribes to refrain from attacking U.S. settlers who moved across their lands on their way to California and Oregon. The treaties also called for the tribes not to attack the eastern tribes who were being moved into Oklahoma.

Among the tribes who were relocated into Oklahoma were the tribes that whites called "the Five Civilized Tribes." These tribes—the Cherokees, the Choctaws, the Chickasaws, the Creeks, and the Seminoles—were called "civilized" because they were the tribes who had adapted the most to European manners of living. Many tribal members from these tribes dressed in European clothes and lived in European-style homes. They farmed and raised cattle and pigs. Between 1830 and 1840, these tribes endured their forced removal into Oklahoma.

In 1854, the Kansas-Nebraska Act reduced the size of Indian Territory when these regions were seized by the U.S. government for white settlement. Large portions of the Dakota regions were also lost, and the parts that did remain in Indian hands belonged mostly to the Sioux peoples. Thus, only Oklahoma remained as a place to send eastern and midwestern Indians. The tribes who previously had reservations in Nebraska and Kansas were moved to Oklahoma. Among those who were moved were the Kickapoos, the Kansas, the Ottawas, the Otos, the Osages, the Missouris, the Miamis, the Shawnees, the Sauks, the Quapaws, the Potawatomis, the Pawnees, the Iowas, the Caddos, the Catawbas, the Illinois, the Cheyennes, and the Arapahos.

The so-called Five Civilized Tribes had been enemies in the East, but in 1859, they formed a loose confederation. During the U.S. Civil War, most of the members of these tribes fought for the Confederacy. As punishment for this action, the U.S. government forced the tribes to give up half of their territory after the war.

After the Civil War, hostile actions also took place in Oklahoma between Indians and U.S. troops. On November 27, 1868, troops under Lt. Colonel George Armstrong Custer attacked Black Kettle and his Cheyenne band on the Washita River without any warning or negotiaton. Black Kettle, a few warriors, and many women and children were killed in the attack.

Oklahoma also became the site to which "hostile" Western Indians were sent if they resisted U.S. seizure of their lands. In 1872–1873, Kintpuash—also known as Captain Jack—led the Modocs against the U.S. Army. Kintpuash and fifty warriors held off one thousand U.S. troops for nearly nine months. When the band finally surrendered, Kintpuash and three other leaders were hanged, and the remaining Modocs were sent to Oklahoma.

In 1877, Chief Joseph and his Nez Perce band left their reservation and began a 1,000-mile (1,600-kilometer) journey to Canada. After the band surrendered, having gotten within 30 miles (48 kilometers) of Canada, they were sent to Oklahoma for six years before being allowed to return to Idaho in 1884. When the Apache leader Goyathlay, or Geronimo, and his band surrendered in 1886, they were sent first to Florida and then to Fort Sill, Oklahoma, where Goyathlay eventually died.

In the 1880s and 1890s, part of Oklahoma was designated as "Unassigned Lands." These lands were the center portion of the state, the Panhandle region, and the area known as Old Greer County. There was also additional pressure to assign more of Oklahoma as land available for "homesteading," the rather innocent-sounding term for the displacement of indigenous peoples by non-Indians seeking a new life and new homes in the West.

After ten years of negotiation, a commission led by U.S. Senator Henry L. Dawes moved to require Indian tribes in Oklahoma to abolish tribal governance and to divide tribal lands for private ownership, first among tribal members and then to non-Native settlers. Indians in Oklahoma protested the Dawes Act (also known as the General Allotment Act) and also protested the attacks on their tribal governments. On July 14, 1905, representatives from each tribe in Oklahoma met at Muskogee and adopted a constitution for an Indian state that they called Sequoyah (after the famed nineteenth-century Cherokee leader who was responsible for developing an alphabet for the Cherokee people). This state would be made up of most of eastern Oklahoma, but it would be a separate, all-Indian state. The Oklahoma Indians petitioned the U.S. Congress for recognition, but the

On National Native Sovereignty Day in 1995, groups of Oklahoma Indians gather in Oklahoma City to protest cuts in services to Native people in the state.

Congress refused to recognize the autonomy of the Indian peoples. Therefore, in 1907, Oklahoma received statehood and was made up of both the Indian and non-Indian portions of the former Oklahoma Indian Territory.

Although only one tribe, the Osages, have maintained a reservation in the state, the Native American presence in Oklahoma is very strong, and dozens of Indian nations are recognized in the state. The following list of recognized Oklahoma tribes was issued by the State of Oklahoma Indian Affairs Commission in 1996: Absentee Shawnee Tribe, Alabama Quassarte, Apache Tribe, Caddo Tribe, Cherokee Nation, Cheyenne-Arapaho Tribe, Chickasaw Nation, Choctaw Nation, Citizen Band of Potawatomi, Comanche Tribe, Delaware Tribe of Eastern Oklahoma, Delaware Tribe of Western Oklahoma, Eastern Shawnee Tribe, Fort Sill Apache Tribe, Iowa Tribe of Oklahoma, Kaw Tribe of Oklahoma, Kialegee Tribal Town, Kickapoo Tribe, Kiowa Tribe, Loyal Shawnee Tribe, Miami Tribe, Modoc Tribe, Muscogee (Creek) Nation, Osage Nation, Oto-Missouria Tribe, Ottawa Tribe, Pawnee Tribe, Peoria Tribe, Ponca Tribe, Quapaw Tribe, Sac and Fox Nation, Seminole Nation, Seneca-Cayuga Tribes, Thlopthlocco Tribal Town, Tonkawa Tribe, United Keetoowah Band of Cherokees, Wichita Tribe, and Wyandotte Tribe.

The 1990 U.S. Census lists 252,420 Oklahoma residents as American Indians, ranking the state first among states in Native American population.

— T. Colonnese

SEE ALSO:

Black Kettle; Captain Jack (Kintpuash); Chief Joseph; Civil War, U.S., Indians in the; Coronado Expedition; Custer, George Armstrong; Dawes Commission; Five Civilized Tribes; General Allotment Act; Geronimo; Indian Trade and Intercourse Acts; Modoc War; Osage;

Removal Act, Indian; Sequoyah; Trail of Tears; Washita, Battle of the.

SUGGESTED READINGS: .

Miner, H. Craig. *The Corporation and the Indian: Tribal Sovereignty and Industrial Civilization in Indian Territory, 1865–1907*. Norman: University of Oklahoma Press, 1988.

O'Brien, Sharon. *American Indian Tribal Governments*. Norman: University of Oklahoma Press, 1989.

Thornton, Russell. *American Indian Holocaust and Survival: A Population History Since 1492*. Norman: University of Oklahoma Press, 1987.

Thornton, Russell. *The Cherokees: A Population History*. Lincoln: University of Nebraska Press, 1990.

Wright, Muriel H. *A Guide to the Indian Tribes of Oklahoma*. Norman: University of Oklahoma Press, 1986.

OLD NORTHWEST

SEE Northwest Ordinance.

OLIVER, LOUIS LITTLECOON (1904–1991)

Creek poet Louis Littlecoon Oliver became one of the most influential contemporary Native American writers relatively late in his life. Oliver, a full-blood Creek of the Alabama tribe of the Muscogee Confederation, was born in Koweta Town, in the Creek Nation, in 1904, three years before Oklahoma statehood. A member of the Raccoon clan, Oliver received the name Littlecoon at birth. According to his own autobiographical accounts, he was given the name Louis Oliver by an Indian agent when Louis's mother refused to reveal his name to a member of the Dawes Commission who was attempting to enroll the family for allotments that would break up Indian Territory (present-day Oklahoma). (Under the terms of the General Allotment Act, Indian lands were to be made available for individual, rather than tribal, ownership, first to Indians and then to non-Indians. One effect of this act was to break up not only the tribal lands but the tribes themselves.)

Orphaned as a child, Oliver was raised by his grandmother and aunts. The federal government put him through the fifth grade, and then on his own he entered the high school at Bacone College, where he graduated in 1926. He studied the work of American and English writers, but he did no publishing until he was nearly eighty years old. Under the influence of many non-Native poets, he was unaware of the idiom of contemporary Native American poetic expression (which is unrhymed free verse). For many years, he attempted poetic expression in iambic pentameter and other such formal poetic constructions, but mostly as a hobby, not seeking to have the work published.

Finally, he was given an opportunity to study the forms of contemporary Native American poetry, by attending a workshop for Native writers where he met some contemporary Native poets and acquired some of their books. He then began writing in the contemporary modes of expression and quickly gained the attention of the community of Native poets throughout the continent when his work began appearing in journals such as *The Greenfield Review*, *Vintage*, *The Beloit Poetry Journal*, *Stone Country*, and *Coyote's Journal*.

Oliver soon published a chapbook (a small book or booklet) of poems entitled *The Horned Snake* (Cross-Cultural Communications, 1982), which was followed shortly by a volume of poetry and prose, *Caught in a Willow Net* (Greenfield Review Press, 1983). In 1990, shortly before his death in 1991, he published *Chasers of the Sun: Creek Indian Thoughts* (Greenfield Review Press).

The esteem in which Oliver is held by his peers was apparent in 1992, when the First Book Awards (a publication prize competition) was inaugurated at a historic conference of nearly four hundred NativeAmerican creative writers at the University of Oklahoma, a conference called Returning the Gift. The First Book Award in prose was designated "The Louis Littlecoon Oliver Memorial Prose Award," a testimony to the late Mr. Oliver that continues in the annual First Book Awards competition.

SEE ALSO:
Bacone College; Creek; Creek Literature, Contemporary; Dawes Commission; First Book Awards; General Allotment Act; Returning the Gift.

OLMEC

In present-day Mexico and Central America, complex civilizations began to organize at about the time that the Roman Empire was expanding across Europe, North Africa, and Palestine. The Olmecs constructed urban areas that were the capitals of politically and socially complex communities, evidence of which exists in the form of residences for the upper classes, stone sculptures, temples, and elaborate tombs.

Shortly after 1500 B.C.E., the Olmec civilization, which provided the founding materials for the Mayas as well as the chain of civilizations that led to the Aztecs in the Valley of Mexico, started organizing complex societies based on the rich wild-food resources of the southern Gulf Coast of present-day Mexico. The Olmec civilization quickly spread across most of Mesoamerica (present-day Central America). In the Olmecs' art, rituals, and other cultural characteristics, one sees the later Maya, Toltec, and Aztec traditions emerging.

By 1400 B.C.E., the first large Olmec settlement rose at a site known today as San Lorenzo, southwest of the Tuxtla Mountains near Mexico's southern Gulf Coast. The settlement contained large public buildings and stone monuments. Evidence, including the probable number of residential sites, indicates that San Lorenzo was a small city in terms of population, but a very large one in terms of economic, political, and religious power across a sizable outlying area.

The elite of San Lorenzo supervised projects involving the moving of hundreds of millions of cubic feet (millions of cubic meters) of earth. Thousands of tons of basalt used to construct monuments were quarried in the Tuxtla Mountains. The San Lorenzo site also has yielded imported obsidian, mica, and other materials from many hundreds of miles (kilometers) away that were used for jewelry, ritual devices, and other prized possessions. It is likely that the Olmecs of San Lorenzo also imported other items, such as foods, that leave little archaeological evidence. Judging from the number of implements recovered for grinding corn (also called maize), it was probably the staple food of the common people at San Lorenzo. The people also probably ate turtles and fish; the elite occasionally dined on young puppies specially raised for that purpose.

The Olmecs did not use metal tools, but they did fashion iron ore into shining disks that the elite wore as ornaments. About 1000 B.C.E., San Lorenzo was surpassed in size by another Olmec settlement, La Venta, east of San Lorenzo, near the Gulf Coast. While La Venta's public and ceremonial areas were larger, its culture was similar to that of San Lorenzo. La Venta reached its peak between 1000 B.C.E. and 750 B.C.E. Other Olmec sites have been identified but have not been widely excavated.

The Olmecs did not occupy Mesoamerica alone; other peoples were also establishing organized societies with agricultural bases at about the same time. In the Valley of Oaxaca, for example, a dozen settlements arose between 1600 and 1300 B.C.E. Later, at about 750 B.C.E., as La Venta declined, the Oaxacan capital of Monte Alban included a civic center with large pyramids, surrounded by rich agricultural land. Olmec sculptures also may contain the earliest hints of hieroglyphic writing, later refined by the Mayas.

As the Olmecs' civilization declined after 600 B.C.E., other groups rose and fell at other sites, each enjoying brief authority over outlying agricultural districts. Each, in turn, organized its society under a religious and military elite, with social classes, rituals, and art forms that continue the tradition that began with the Olmecs and ended with the Aztecs.

SEE ALSO:
Aztec; Central America, Indigenous Peoples of; Maya; Mexico, Indigenous Peoples of; Toltec.

OMAHA

Omaha is an anglicized name for U'ma'ha, the Native people who occupied the eastern portion of the area that is today called the state of Nebraska. Omaha, the largest city in the state, is named after the U'ma'has. Today, the Omahas occupy a small reservation about sixty miles (ninety-seven kilometers) north of the city of Omaha. Among other things, the Omahas are known as the originators of the modern powwow format. Their history includes several notable individuals, such as Big Elk, the Omahas' last hereditary chief; several members of the LaFlesche family; and Rodney Grant,

A colossal head carved by Olmecs in the ancient settlement at La Venta, in Mexico. The carving is on display at La Venta Archaeology Museum in present-day Villa Hermosa, in the state of Tabasco, Mexico.

A group of Omaha women caring for their children as they pound corn into meal, braid husks, and work a small loom. This engraving, done in the late 1890s, also depicts the Omahas' earth lodge dwellings.

an actor who starred in the movie *Dances with Wolves.*

During the 1870s and 1880s, the Omahas sheltered a group of Poncas led by Standing Bear who were returning to their homeland along the Niobrara River (along Nebraska's northern border) against the orders of the U. S. Army. Several prominent Omahas, most notably the LaFlesche family, worked on a nationwide publicity campaign to nullify army orders that had sent the Poncas to Indian Territory (later called Oklahoma). The Omahas and Standing Bear were instrumental in the handing down of a significant federal court ruling in Omaha. Handed down in 1879, the ruling held that Indians should be treated as "persons" under United States law. This was the first ruling of its kind; it was aimed at keeping the army from moving Indians to Indian Territory without legal cause.

Francis LaFlesche (Zhogaxe) (c. 1867–1932) was one of the Omahas' leaders in Standing Bear's defense. After the trial, LaFlesche attended National University Law School, in Washington, D.C., graduating in 1892. While there, he began working with anthropologist Alice C. Fletcher and collaborated with her on *A Study of Omaha Music* (1893). Fletcher and LaFlesche also collaborated on *The Omaha Tribe* (1911), published a year after he joined the Bureau of American Ethnology. Francis LaFlesche also authored *Middle Five: Indian Boys at School* (1900), a play titled *Da-o-ma* (1912), *Who Was the Medicine Man?* (1904), and *A Dictionary of the Osage Language* (1932).

During the late nineteenth century, the Omahas were split between traditionalists and progressives. The LaFlesche home—a two-story frame house—stood in a settlement that the traditionals scorned as "The Home of the Make Believe White Men." The Omahas had become United States citizens under the Dawes (Allotment) Act in 1887. They were one of the first Native American peoples to divide their lands under that law, and the "choice" of private versus tribal landownership under the General Allotment Act was one that divided many Native peoples.

Susan LaFlesche (1865–1915) became a government doctor on the Omaha reservation during a time when cholera, influenza, tuberculosis, and other diseases were reaching epidemic proportions. She blazed a career of genius through a number of white schools, and then she nearly worked herself to death serving the Omahas as a government physician from 1889 until her death in 1915.

LaFlesche became one of a handful of Native American physicians in the nineteenth century—a handful that includes Charles Eastman and Carlos Montezuma. The hospital that Susan LaFlesche built at Walthill has since been declared a national historic landmark. Since 1988, her memory has been celebrated at an annual festival there.

A nineteenth-century portrait of an Omaha tribal leader identified as Ong Pa Ton Ga.

See also:
Big Elk; Bureau of American Ethnology; Dawes Commission; Eastman, Charles; General Allotment Act; Montezuma, Carlos; Nebraska; Oklahoma; Picotte-LaFlesche, Susan; Ponca.

OÑATE EXPEDITION

For the Pueblo peoples of the upper Rio Grande Valley and other Native peoples in adjacent areas, life took a grim turn when the Spanish decided to conquer and permanently colonize New Mexico at the end of the sixteenth century. The Pueblos had suffered the disruptions of five previous Spanish expeditions—those of Francisco Vásquez de Coronado in the 1540s, Fray Agustín Rodríguez and Francisco Sánchez Chamuscado in 1581, Fray Bernardino Beltrán and Antonio de Espejo in 1582, Gaspar Castaño de Sosa in 1589, and Francisco Leyva de Bonilla and Antonio Gutiérrez de Umaña in 1593. These expeditions had only visited the country briefly and then had returned to New Spain (present-day Mexico) or, in the case of the last expedition, met death while venturing on to the Great Plains. But on January 26, 1598, a large expedition led by Juan de Oñate left northern New Spain with royal authorization to permanently occupy New Mexico by conquest.

The Oñate expedition included 129 soldiers, some with their families, eighty-three wagons, seven thousand head of livestock, and 8 Franciscan priests. Oñate's contract with the Spanish Crown required him to pay for all of the expenses of the conquest and occupation out of his own pocket; he would have to try to recoup his investment from the land and its peoples. He was granted the titles of governor and captain-general and given the authorization to grant encomiendas to his companions. (*Encomienda* was a system of forced labor enacted against Native peoples by their Spanish conquerors.) He also received an encomienda allowing the forced labor of a large number of Indians for himself and his heirs for three generations.

The conquest of the Pueblos was brutal. The first sign of serious resistance was at Acoma, where the Acomas had killed Juan de Zaldívar and his detachment of soldiers. Oñate allowed Zaldívar's brother, a vengeful Vicente de Zaldívar, to bring in field artillery and batter the pueblo. A large number of Acomas were punished by having one of their feet chopped off, and hundreds of them were led off into captivity. With this example of Spanish intent, no other Pueblos offered resistance, and the Spanish soon took control of the region. The disruption to the cultures and economies of the Native people was incalculable. Not for another eight decades would the Pueblos be able to mount a serious threat to Spanish rule, in the Pueblo Revolt of 1680.

Though the Oñate expedition brought a permanent Spanish presence to New Mexico, it ruined Oñate both financially and professionally. His colonists proved unruly and demanded that he abandon the enterprise. When he refused, they lodged serious charges against him regarding his conduct, which were sent to the viceroy of New Spain. The priests also made serious charges against him. He exhausted his wealth on the enterprise and wasted much of his time in a vain search for gold. In 1609, Oñate lost the benefits of his contract and was replaced as governor by Don Pedro de Peralta, and New Mexico became a royal colony maintained at crown expense.

SEE ALSO:
Acoma Pueblo; Coronado Expedition; Encomienda; New Mexico; New Spain; Pueblo; Pueblo Revolt of 1680.

ONEIDA

The Oneidas, one of the five original nations of the Iroquois Confederacy (with the Mohawks, Onondagas, Cayugas, and Senecas), occupied an area in upstate New York east of present-day Syracuse. Their nation was adjacent to the Mohawks on their east and the Onondagas on the west. By the late twentieth century, the tribe's landholdings had been reduced to about thirty square miles (seventy-eight square kilometers).

The Oneidas are the smallest of the five nations in the confederacy that the English called the Five Nations, the French called the Iroquois, and Native people themselves called Haudenosaunee, meaning "People of the Longhouse." The Oneidas are regarded with the Cayugas as "Younger Brothers" in the confederacy, in which the "Older Brothers" are the Seneca (at the "western door" of the symbolic national longhouse) and Mohawks (at the "eastern door"). The Onondagas have the role of firekeepers, or executive officers.

The Oneidas were a semisedentary people who produced food from maize (corn), squashes, and beans. Their diet was supplemented by hunting. They lived in communal longhouses that contained extended families of matrilineal descent, and the tribe was divided into three clans.

In the 1600s, the Oneidas had one principal town, which included about eight longhouses, or perhaps four hundred to five hundred people. The town was destroyed by a French-Canadian expedition in 1696. Shortly after that, the Oneidas provided land to Tuscaroras who moved from present-day North Carolina to become the sixth nation of the Iroquois Confederacy.

Not until the American Revolution had members of the Iroquois Confederacy ever gone to war with each other. The Oneidas supported the patriots in the American Revolution; their principal chief, Skenandoah, supplied food and other aid to George Washington's troops during a desperate winter at Valley Forge. The Mohawks, however, were supporters of the British in the Revolution and, under Joseph Brant, often raided the Oneidas. After the Revolution, some of the Oneidas moved to Thames River, Ontario, while others moved to Green Bay, Wisconsin.

In addition to Skenandoah, many Oneidas have been prominent from the United States' early history to the present. The Oneida chief Grasshopper was a confidant of James Madison. Frederick J. Dockstader, the anthropologist and historian, is of Oneida and Navajo descent. In our own time, Oneida folksinger Joanne Shenandoah has earned

A family photograph of an Oneida couple identified as "Israel Hill and Wife, Oneida, Wisconsin, 1909." In the early 1800s, facing the loss of tribal lands through land deals and treaties in New York State, many Oneidas (original members of the Iroquois Confederacy) chose to resettle in Wisconsin near Green Bay, where they live today.

a national reputation, as has actor Graham Greene, who played a leading role in the movie *Dances with Wolves*. About five thousand Oneidas lived in the United States late in the twentieth century.

See also:
American Revolution; Greene, Graham; Iroquois Confederacy; Longhouse; Mohawk; New York; Onondaga; Shenandoah, Joanne; Skenandoah; Tuscarora.

ONONDAGA

The Onondagas are one of the five original nations of the Iroquois Confederacy (along with the Mohawks, Cayugas, Oneidas, and Senecas). Located in central upstate New York near present-day Syracuse, the Onondagas act as keepers of the Iroquois's traditional central council fire and as executives in the Iroquois Confederacy.

According to Iroquois legend, the Onondagas were the last of the five nations to agree to the Great Peace proposed by Hiawatha and Deganawidah the Peacemaker. The evil wizard Tadadaho, who had long frustrated the plans of the Peacemaker and Hiawatha, was an Onondaga. The origin story of the Iroquois League describes the years-long struggle during which Tadadaho, with his snake-encrusted head, frustrated attempts to bring peace to the Iroquois. When Tadadaho finally agreed to recognize the Great Law of Peace, his name was given to the council's chief executive officer as proof, to the Iroquois, of the triumph of peace over war and good over evil.

Today, the Iroquois Grand Council meets in a simple log structure at Nedrow, south of Syracuse, on Onondaga ancestral lands. Every five years in that cabin, Jake Thomas recites the entire Great Law of Peace in its original language. Thomas was the only person alive in the late twentieth century who could recite the whole story from his memory, with aid from several wampum belts that record history for the Onondagas and other Iroquois. The recitation usually takes Thomas, who is a Cayuga, three days.

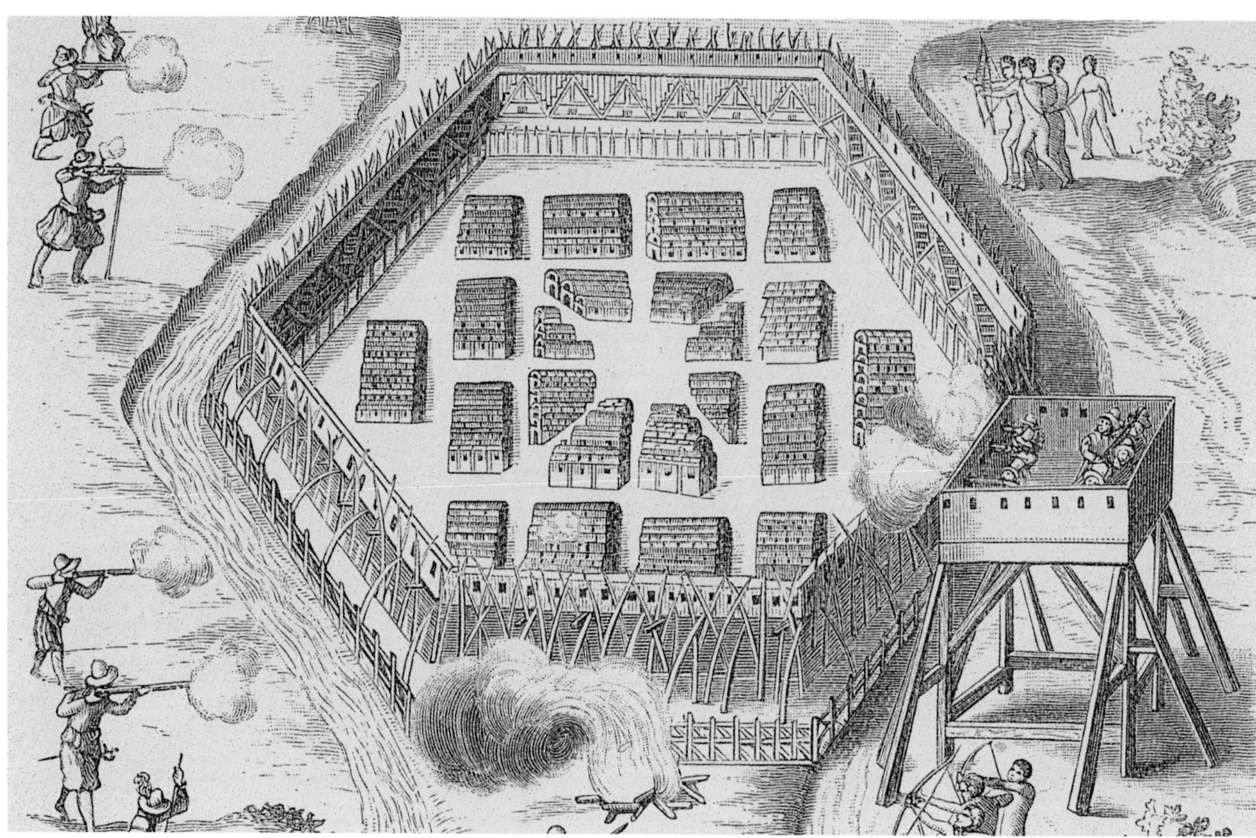

This engraving of an Onondaga settlement depicts a cluster of longhouses within a fortlike enclosure. Outside the fort, various hostile forces, both Native and European, lay siege to the inhabitants with a variety of weapons and other equipment.

Lake Onondaga, which figures prominently in the origin story of the Iroquois League, today is surrounded by Syracuse and its suburbs. The lake is polluted, and most fish taken from it may not be safely eaten. Syracuse and its suburbs figure in one of the more dramatic of many Iroquois land claims in upstate New York. By the mid-1990s, the Onondagas were considering a court test of their claim to lands now occupied by Syracuse and its suburbs, due to fraudulent practices by land speculators and New York State two centuries earlier.

SEE ALSO:
Deganawidah; Hiawatha; Iroquois Confederacy; Mohawk; Oneida; Wampum.

ON-RESERVATION BOARDING SCHOOLS

SEE Boarding Schools.

ONTARIO

Ontario, Canada's second-largest province, is bounded by Hudson Bay to the north, the province of Manitoba to the west, the province of Quebec to the east, and, to the south, the Great Lakes region, including small portions of the U.S. states of Minnesota, Michigan, and New York. Ontario occupies 412,581 square miles (1,072,711 square kilometers), and its capital is Toronto. The national capital is also located in Ontario at Ottawa, which makes Ontario the demographic, economic, and political center of Canada.

In historic times, Ontario was a woodland area occupied primarily by the Ojibwe (Chippewa) and Cree people. The Algonquians and Wyandots (Hurons) also made their homes within modern Ontario boundaries. The Ojibwes and Crees trapped furs in the winter; they hunted, gathered, and fished during better weather, using canoes as transportation. Native peoples used birch bark to make canoes and containers and to cover the dome-shaped dwellings that they built. Artistic and decorative traditions abounded, as evidenced by unique rock paintings in Ontario. With the advent of the fur trade, the Crees and Ojibwes supplied trading posts with furs in exchange for European trade goods. Increasing dependence on European trade goods with a corresponding decrease in the availability of furs led to an economic imbalance between the Natives and settlers. Gradually, the individual bands signed treaties and moved onto reserves.

Today, Ontario contains 182 reserves totaling 1,727,989 acres (691,196 hectares). In 1986, 26,135 people lived on reserves in Ontario, while 141,220 people of aboriginal (Native) origin lived off-reserve in Ontario. Reserve economics typically revolves around commercial fishing, wild rice gathering, and sales of handicrafts and art. One major development has been the distinctive Woodlands art style pioneered by Norval Morrisseau, an Ojibwe from northern Ontario. This internationally acclaimed artistic style draws on and reinforces the traditions of the Cree and Ojibwe people.

At issue in the increasingly urbanized areas of Ontario—particularly in the southern portions of the province, near the U.S. border—has been the toxic pollution of waterways used by Native people. The incidence of mercury in the English–Wabigoon River system of northwestern Ontario triggered a court battle that resulted in a multimillion dollar settlement for two Ojibwe bands in 1985. The money won in the suit went to aid people who had been affected by mercury poisoning.

SEE ALSO:
Ojibwe; Wyandot (Huron).

ORAL HISTORY

Oral history is a way to explore the history of a people and culture through interviews with individuals. Oral history interviews are often conducted with individuals who witnessed and experienced the activities of a particular era but themselves were usually the ordinary participants in events, not the leaders or famous people. An oral history narrative is a concentrated reminiscence guided by someone who should be a sympathetic student of history or culture. It is meant to be preserved, either by being written down, recorded through sound or video technology, or both.

An undated photo of Native residents near the Fort William settlement in the Thunder Bay area of Ontario.

A drummer sings into the microphone at a powwow on the Confederated Siletz reservation in northwest Oregon. The Confederated Tribes of Siletz consist of twenty-four separate tribes with a common Siletz Tribal Council.

On August 23, 1954, Congress passed the Western Oregon Termination Act, which called for the federal government to suspend recognition and services to every tribe and band in western Oregon within two years. Called the "Termination Era," this period in U.S.-Indian relations was to have a disastrous effect on Oregon tribes. Among its consequences were tribal land sales, an end to the federal-Indian trust relationship, an end to federal tribal programs, and an end to tribal sovereignty. In 1970, the philosophy of termination was formally repudiated by President Richard M. Nixon. In a message to Congress, Nixon asked for a resolution that "would expressly renounce, repudiate and repeal the termination policy." Federal restoration of the individual tribes came about gradually, but with it, treaty obligations were once again established. By the end of the twentieth century, the following tribes have achieved federal recognition.

A young participant at a tribal powwow on the Confederated Siletz Reservation in Oregon.

The Confederated Tribes of Warm Springs have a 641,035-acre (246,414-hectare) reservation in central Oregon, just east of Mt. Hood. Their tribal membership of 3,405 includes the Warm Springs (or Tenino), the Wasco, and the Northern Paiute Nations. Their famed Kah-Nee-Ta Resort, which boasts over three hundred days of sunshine per year, is the centerpiece of several economically successful tribal enterprises. Their tribal offices are located in Warm Springs.

The Confederated Tribes of the Umatilla Indian Reservation tribal enrollment of 1,494 includes descendants of the Cayuse, Umatilla, and Walla Walla tribes. Their northeastern Oregon reservation was opened to non-Indian settlement by the federal government and today incorporates a scattered arrangement of 157,982 acres (63,193 hectares). Their tribal headquarters is located in Pendleton.

The Confederated Tribes of Siletz successfully won federal restoration status in 1977. Their tribal enrollment of 2,180 encompasses descendants from the Alsea, Chastacosta, Chetco, Chinook, Kusa, Siuslaw, Shasta, Umpqua, Macanotin, Joshua, Coquille, Tututni, Molalla, Tillamook, Rogue River, Dekubetde, Kwatami, Galice Creek, Salmon River, Kalapuya, Naltnatunne, Yaquina, Yuki, and Klickitat tribes, all of western Oregon. Their 3,666-acre (1,466-hectare) reservation is located in Lincoln County, in northwest Oregon. The tribe provides a wide variety of services to its members and other Indians in an eleven-county service area through three tribal offices, located in Siletz, Portland, and Salem (which is also the capital of the state of Oregon).

Devil's Gate and the Sweetwater River, on the Oregon Trail in Wyoming. Many Euro-American immigrants thought of themselves as bringing "civilization" to this part of North America; but the ground covered by the trail was part of a network of trade and commerce that Native inhabitants had used for centuries before the arrival of any Europeans.

The best-known account of the Oregon Trail was written by Francis Parkman, a historian who traveled the route himself and witnessed the difficulties of pioneer life, as well as encounters with Native peoples along the way. The book, titled *The Oregon Trail,* was published in 1849, only a few years after the Oregon Trail became active, just as traffic was swelling with the discovery of gold in California. Parkman had traveled the trail in 1846 and published parts of the book in magazines during 1847 and 1848. Ironically, Parkman was almost forced to give up on the trip, as well as his writing plans, after he became lost on the prairies of Kansas at the beginning of his trek.

Parkman did find the trail again as it emerged into areas in which Native Americans lived independently. He wrote of his travels in areas controlled by the Pawnee, Sioux, Northern Cheyennes, Arapahos, and other Native Americans. He spent two weeks living in an Oglala Lakota (Sioux) village. Most of Parkman's story concerned the European-American pioneers along the trail, whom he regarded as bringing civilization to the wilderness.

SEE ALSO:

Gold Rush; Mexican-American War.

ORTIZ, SIMON J. (1941–)

Simon J. Ortiz was born and raised in the Acoma Pueblo community in Albuquerque, New Mexico. He was schooled within the Bureau of Indian Affairs on the Acoma Reservation. After high school, he attended the University of Iowa, where he was a student in the International Writing Program and eventually earned a master's degree in writing.

A marker along the Oregon Trail at a section in Wyoming called South Pass.

Ortiz has written many books, including *A Good Journey*, *Woven Stone*, *After and Before the Lightning*, and *From Sand Creek*, which won a Pushcart Prize in 1982. He was invited to the White House in 1980, where he was honored as a participant in the president's "Salute to Poetry and American Poets." Besides writing poetry and short stories, Ortiz has also written a book especially for young readers entitled *The People Shall Continue*. His poems have been published in several poetry collections, including *Songs from This Earth on Turtle's Back*, *Harper's Anthology of 20th Century Native American Poetry*, and *Durable Breath: Contemporary Native American Poetry*.

This photo, taken in 1923, shows two young Osage Indians at a festival celebrating the tribe's receipt of millions of dollars in payment by the U.S. government for rights to oil on Osage land.

Simon J. Ortiz has taught creative writing and Native American literature at San Diego State University in California and at the University of New Mexico. He is the father of three children, Raho, Rainy, and Sara, and he currently lives in Tucson, Arizona.

See also:
Acoma Pueblo.

OSAGE

The Osages, a Siouan-language group who were originally one with the Omahas, Poncas, Kansas, and Quapaws, lived in an area that is now known as Missouri. While they were primarily a stable farming tribe, they occasionally went to the eastern Plains to hunt.

In 1821, Missouri became a state, and the Osages were removed to Kansas, where they received a portion of their old hunting grounds. By the late 1870s, the Osages were being intruded upon by other Native nations and settlers alike, and the government's Indian office struck an agreement with the tribe for the exchange of their Kansas lands for a rich tract of land in Indian Territory (present-day Oklahoma).

During the allotment era of the late 1890s, Congress forced tribes to give up their lands—initially for individual Indian ownership and then for settlement by non-Indians. Like other tribal groups, the Osages reluctantly accepted the division of their lands into allotments for individuals and their families, as mandated by the Dawes Commission—with one major exception. The Osages managed to maintain their tribal mineral rights.

This exception to the general rule of allotment became a critical difference when oil was discovered on the Oklahoma Osage Reservation in 1897, turning their land into one of the greatest oil fields in the world. Those who were on the tribal rolls at the time were called "headright hold-

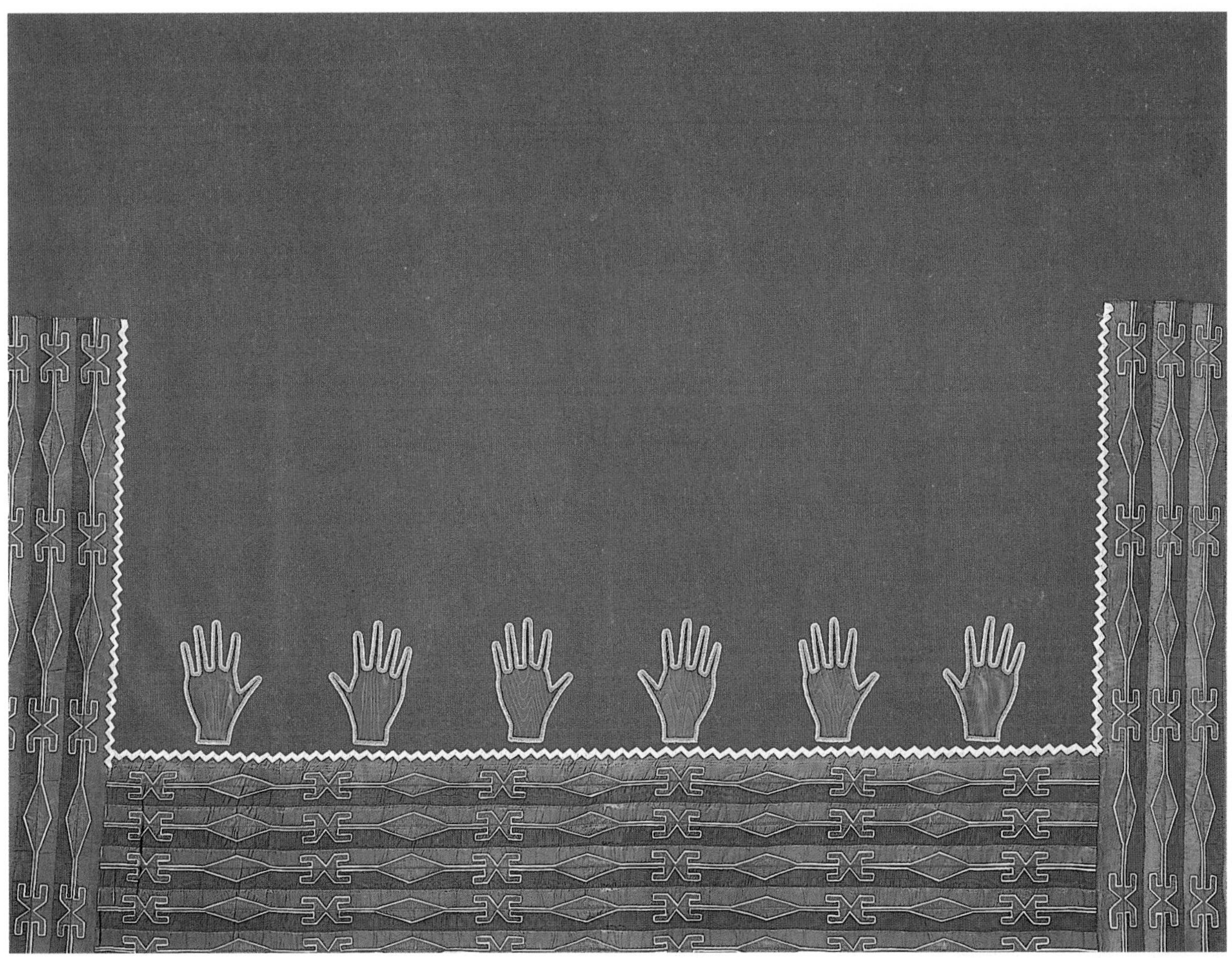

A beautiful wool Osage wearing blanket from around 1900. Decorated with ribbon and featuring six beaded hands, this blanket is for sale at a Santa Fe, New Mexico, art gallery.

ers." The returns from this discovery were considerable—they added up to about $20 million per year—and made some Osages the wealthiest American Indian people in North America. But others were tricked into selling their land to dishonest non-Natives, and beginning in about 1921, the Osages lived in terror as non-Indians conspired to obtain this wealth. In a three-year period, there were twenty-four unsolved murder cases, and a great number of Osage people died conspicuously. Shootings, poisonings, and even the blowing up of houses became the norm for that time, which was noted as a "reign of terror" among people in Oklahoma.

Strangely, when a wealthy Osage was found murdered, usually a non-Indian was named as the inheritor. And there were numerous deaths ruled as suicide that have left families wondering about the true reasons for the deaths.

In 1925, Congress gave the Osage Agency guardianship of the headright fortunes. The Osages became wealthy and used their money to develop self-direction for their nation. During the 1950s, when tribal status for many Native American nations was being terminated, the Osages narrowly escaped termination by Congress. Had the Osage tribe been terminated, their mineral estate would have been divided up among various corporations.

When they were removed into Oklahoma in the 1800s, the Osages had developed a constitution. Only headright holders were allowed to vote, and the vote was not one-person, one-vote, but depended upon the number of headrights one held. This put most of the political power into the hands of those with the greatest wealth. To add further to the influence held by the wealthy, only headright holders could sit on the council.

Two Osage representatives are escorted by the commissioner of the Indian Affairs Office in Washington, D.C., in 1923. Fifty Osage tribal members met with President Warren G. Harding to discuss Osage oil properties in Oklahoma.

In 1993, the Osages voted to change the Osage government and constitution. The vote came after a suit was filed against the federal government to force a change. The judge in the case established an Osage Commission to find out what the Osage people wanted to do about their government. The Osages chose a constitutional form of government, and so they drew up a constitution that set out the rights and responsibilities of the people and their government. The people also voted to have two councils—one, the Osage Tribal Council, to govern the mineral estate and headright holders' interests, and another, the Osage National Council, to maintain the everyday governmental functions of the tribe except dealings with the mineral estate.

The Osages also chose to have a one-person, one-vote rule. The Osage Commission had to search worldwide for all eligible Osage voters and counted almost eleven thousand. The commission even found Osage people as far away as Australia. The voters registered with the Osage Commission and at an appointed time were given questions to answer. The answers to these questions produced responses that were similar to those resulting from a vote. The Osage Commission figured that about 60 percent of the Osages participating in this process had not been eligible to vote under the former Osage government.

On February 4, 1994, about 65 percent of the Osages voted to adopt their new constitution and reform their government. Their Constitution of 1881 had been declared obsolete by the United States government, but the old constitution was nonetheless used as a base for the new one. The 1994 Constitution allows for changes to be made; this is expected to happen as the people become more involved in their government.

The Osages also agreed not to set a blood quantum (or minimum percentage of Indian blood) for eligibility for enrollment, and with the new laws and the new government, more Osages are expected to begin enrolling with the tribe. A general election was conducted on June 6, 1994.

The Osage Nation headquarters is in Pawhuska, Oklahoma.

— S. S. Davis

SEE ALSO:
Dawes Commission; General Allotment Act; Oklahoma; Omaha; Ponca; Tallchief, Maria; Termination Policy.

OSCEOLA
(1804–1838)

An engraving of Seminole leader Osceola and his followers being arrested by U.S. soldiers in 1837. Osceola died in prison several months later.

Osceola is best known for his defiant refusal to leave his homeland in Florida. His fight to protect his tribal land from European-American encroachment earned him distinction as a brilliant military leader. As such, Osceola helped the Seminoles outmaneuver the United States Army and Florida militia in the Second Seminole War, which lasted from 1835 to 1842.

Osceola was born close to the Tallapossa River, near the present-day Alabama-Georgia border. His mother was Polly Copinger, a mixed-blood Creek, and his father was thought to be a Scotch trader named William Powell. Osceola, known as Billy Powell to non-Indian people, considered himself a full-blood.

Around 1815, Osceola and his mother escaped to Florida to avoid the large Creek removal to Indian Territory (present-day Oklahoma) and eventually settled with the Seminoles at Peas Creek. As he grew into manhood, Osceola began to display his abilities as a hunter and fighter and rose to leadership among a small band of Tallassees, who called him Tustenuggee.

The Treaty of Camp Moultrie established a reservation for the Seminoles to live undisturbed and in peace. Once the reservation was established, Osceola and his mother left Peas Creek to live with the other Seminoles. Here, he worked as a police officer for the United States government, mainly to protect Seminoles from non-Indian intruders.

In April 1835, Indian agent Wiley Thompson forced the Seminoles to sign a new treaty that required them to move to Indian Territory. Osceola reportedly stuck a dagger through the middle of the document and refused to sign it. Shortly afterward, Thompson had him arrested for his defiant behavior and released him when he agreed to sign the treaty.

To avoid removal, Osceola and other Seminoles hid in the swamplands and began an aggressive campaign against forced removal by the U.S. government and the Florida militia. With their knowledge of the terrain, the Seminoles used the swamplands to fight their wars and to protect them from federal and state armies.

An illustration portraying two Ottawa leaders near Lake Huron, which lies between present-day New York State and Ontario, Canada. As members of the Great Huron Trade Circle, the Ottawas supplied furs to French traders in Quebec in exchange for such European goods as cloth, beads, paints, kettles, and knives.

The Ottawas became well known as traders, particularly because their territory was a crossroads for trade between many Indian peoples. With trade came a political role as builders of alliances. Pontiac was perhaps the Ottawas' best-known confederacy builder. Later, some branches of the Ottawas joined in several tribal alliances, the largest assembled by Tecumseh, that attempted to stop Euro-American settlement in the Ohio Valley. Ottawa traders and diplomats ranged an area that encompassed the entire chain of the Great Lakes, as well as nearby areas of Ontario and Quebec.

At home, the Ottawas lived in agricultural villages during the summer and split into nomadic hunting bands during the long cold winters. With the coming of French traders, many Ottawas became part of the fur-trading economy. Women tended the fields and hearth, and men attended to most of the hunting, trading, and diplomacy. The Ottawas had a clan system that provided unity between four or five major groups made up of roughly twenty smaller bands.

The Ottawa Pontiac organized a large intertribal alliance with the Ojibwes, Potawatomis, and others in an effort to check the expansion of British influence into their territories. Britain was moving in to take forts abandoned by the French in the French and Indian War (1754–1763). During Pontiac's War (1763–1764), the tribal confederation captured eight of the British army's twelve forts before British reinforcements turned the military tide.

In 1764, Colonel Henry Bouquet led fifteen hundred armed men in a final show of force at the

Indian alliance's major camp in present-day Ohio. Instead of facing severe losses, Native leaders agreed to sue for peace. Pontiac was not present at this meeting with Bouquet, however, and did not agree to stop the war until the next year. Meeting with trader and British emissary George Croghan, Pontiac agreed to peace only if Indian lands would be protected. Croghan promised this, as he tapped the rum keg generously for Pontiac. A treaty of peace was concluded in 1766, after which Pontiac was ridiculed by many of his people for giving too much in compromise. He was ultimately forced into exile .

The Ottawas have also left a mark on the Catholic Church. In 1832, William Blackbird, an Ottawa, was summoned to a seminary in Rome as the first American Indian candidate for the Roman Catholic priesthood. He studied for two years but died suddenly on the eve of his ordination. Ottawa historian Alexander Blackbird speculated that William Blackbird had been murdered to keep an Indian from becoming a priest. The first Native American priest was Albert Negahnquet, a Potawatomi, who was ordained in 1903.

See also:
Algonquian; Canada, Native–Non-Native Relations in; French and Indian War; Ojibwe; Ontario; Pontiac; Pontiac's War; Potawatomi; Tecumseh.

OWENS, LOUIS (1948–)

In his work for the U.S. Forest Service and in his many literary pursuits, Louis Owens has shown a great understanding of and affection for wilderness lands.

Louis Owens is a novelist and scholar of Choctaw, Cherokee, and Irish descent. Currently a professor of English at the University of New Mexico, he was born in Lompoc, California, in 1948 and grew up in both Mississippi and California. Following a seven-year seasonal career with the U.S. Forest Service as a wilderness ranger and firefighter, he received a Ph.D. in literature from the University of California at Davis in 1981.

Owens has published numerous essays on subjects ranging from Native American and mainstream American literature to backpacking and fishing. His published books include the novels *Wolfsong* (1991), *The Sharpest Sight* (1992), and *Bone Game* (1994), as well as the following critical works: *American Indian Novelists* (with Tom Colonnese, 1985), *John Steinbeck's Re-Vision of America* (1985), *The Grapes of Wrath: Trouble in the Promised Land* (1989), and *Other Destinies: Understanding the American Indian Novel* (1992). Currently, Owens serves with Gerald Vizenor as the coeditor of the American Indian Literature and Critical Studies series for the University of Oklahoma Press.

See also:
Vizenor, Gerald.

PACIFIC SALMON TREATY

The Pacific Salmon Treaty, signed in 1985, is an agreement between the government of Canada, the government of the United States (which includes under its jurisdiction the states of Alaska, Washington, and Oregon), and the Indian tribes of the Pacific Northwest. The purpose of the treaty is to conserve and manage the harvest of five species of Pacific salmon.

A somewhat romanticized view of Native people spearfishing at night by torchlight. Tribal fishing rights have long occupied the energies and passions of Indian groups in the Pacific Northwest.

Pacific salmon form the basis of a major industry that provides a large number of jobs in the Northwest. Many of these jobs are on commercial fishing boats, and some are shore-based jobs for cannery workers and other workers involved in the processing of the salmon catch. Pacific salmon is also a valuable resource for Indian tribes who fish for subsistence and ceremonial purposes. In addition to the commercial fishing business and tribal uses of salmon, recreational fishing has become a big business. In the years leading up to the Pacific Salmon Treaty, with so many interests and the danger of a shrinking resource, cooperative planning regarding the salmon became necessary.

Accomplishing the primary purpose of the treaty—managing and conserving the Pacific salmon population—is complicated because of the salmon's life cycle. The fish begin their lives in freshwater, migrate to the sea, and eventually return to freshwater to spawn. In the course of its life, a salmon travels through a number of jurisdictions, making it difficult for parties to agree on a management plan.

For the past several decades, the United States and Canada have discussed management of the salmon resource, but it was not until certain species began to decline in number that attempts to make a cooperative plan became serious. In 1982, the two countries met and negotiated what became the core of the final treaty, which was signed in 1985. The treaty created a commission and several panels. Members of these groups—which oversee the effort to conserve and manage the salmon—include representatives from the United States and Canada as well as representatives from Pacific Northwest Indian tribes.

SEE ALSO:
Fishing Rights.

A group of Native fishermen pull in salmon during a 1966 "fish-in" on the Nisqually River in Olympia, Washington. These and other Pacific Northwest Indians are concerned with their right to abide by tribal rules rather than state wildlife regulations on tribal land and whether non-Indians should be allowed to hunt and fish on reservation land.

PADDLE TO SEATTLE

In the first gathering of canoeists and craftspeople known as "Paddle to Seattle," members of seventeen coastal Indian tribes created dugout canoes, converging on the metropolitan area of Seattle, Washington, from their communities along Puget Sound, the Strait of Juan de Fuca, and the coast of the Pacific Ocean. This event, which took place in conjunction with the state of Washington's centennial in 1989, revived the art of making and sailing dugout canoes that once were the major mode of transportation among indigenous peoples of the area.

The first Paddle to Seattle was followed, in the spring of 1993, by an even more grueling test of the canoes and canoeists—a 1,000-mile (1,600-kilometer) journey from the Puget Sound area of Washington to Bella Bella, British Columbia, the route winding northwestward along the Pacific Coast through the Inland Passage. The journey, undertaken to illustrate the community nature of cultural revival, took a month and was organized to observe the Year of Indigenous Peoples declared by the United Nations. Participants called the journey *Enatai on Alki,* meaning "a crossing into the future" in the Chinook language.

Fifteen paddlers set out in two canoes from La Push, on the northern coast of Washington, on May 25, 1993. One canoe carried six Quileute tribal members; the other carried the rest. Two support boats accompanied the canoes with camping gear and food. A U.S. Coast Guard escort followed the four craft as they plunged into choppy seas along a sandbar near La Push. The night before, the Quileute community of La Push had celebrated the beginning of the journey with singing, dancing, and a dinner of salmon.

The canoeists represented the Hoh, Makah, Jamestown Klallam, Port Gamble Klallam, Suquamish, and Duwamish tribes. The Quileutes led the way. Not all of the participants were coastal Indians; the "Canoe Nations," as they call themselves, also accepted non-Indian paddlers as well as Indians from other areas of North America.

At the end of their monthlong journey, the participants celebrated Washington State Day in Bella Bella, British Columbia, Canada. This was one of many events in a weeklong potlatch there between June 27 and July 3. Several thousand indigenous people, including guests from as far away as New Zealand, attended the potlatch.

In 1989, the Quileutes sent a canoe to Puget Sound as part of the Paddle to Seattle, a 340-mile (544-kilometer) round trip. David Forlines, a Quileute traditionalist, carver, and storyteller, inspired the Quileutes' revival of arts related to the making and sailing of dugout canoes. He died in 1991 at the age of forty-five, but many of the participants in the journey to Bella Bella in 1993 credited him for inspiring them as well. Emmett Oliver, a Quinault Indian and a member of Washington State's maritime commission, also was influential in reviving the art of canoe making as well as the ceremonies connected with the craft. Oliver supervised a Native American Canoe Project beginning in 1987, in which canoe-making skills were taught. Some of the sea craft constructed as part of this project were as long as seventy feet (twenty meters).

SEE ALSO:
Canoes; Duwamish; Giveaway; Makah; Port Gamble Klallum; Quileute; Quinault; Suquamish Tribe of the Port Madison Reservation; Washington Coast and Puget Sound Indians, History of; Washington State.

PAIUTE

In early times, life for the Paiutes of the Great Basin often consisted of a continuous search for food and water. The harsh desert environment of their homeland and its lack of resources forced the Paiutes to commute inside their tribal territories in order to survive. Although the Paiutes who occupied the high plateau around the Grand Canyon and in southern Utah grew maize (corn), because there was not enough rainfall to grow crops, the Paiutes were primarily hunters and gatherers. With each changing season, the Paiute families journeyed to new areas of the desert in search of food. In winter, they hunted fish and game. In spring, they ate roots, plants, seeds, fowl, and fish. In summer, they moved on to areas where they could find seeds, rice grass, berries, rodents, snakes, and ducks. In fall, pine nuts and rabbits made up a good portion of their diet.

McKay Pikyavit, leader of the Kanosh band of the Paiute Tribe of Utah. Like many Paiutes today, he is involved in farming for a living.

Rabbit skins were also important to the Paiutes as warm clothing against the frigid winter winds. The rabbit pelts were cut into continuous spiral strips and then twisted into ropes. The ropes were then sewn together to make a robe-coat. They wore these robes throughout winter and fall. In contrast, the Paiutes' clothing was minimal during the summer's great heat. The Paiutes were also highly skilled at making vessels that could hold water and at making finely twined and coiled baskets used to gather and store seeds.

The Paiutes lived in small family units because there was not enough food in any one place to feed a larger group. A man might have two wives; if the number of women was low, however, a woman might have two husbands. Individual families would only mass together in one location if, for some unusual reason, there was an abundance of food found there. But this was rare.

The tribe was divided into two divisions. Northern Paiutes lived in the areas now known as Oregon, Idaho, Nevada, and California. These Indians were also known as Paviotsos. Southern Paiutes occupied Utah, Arizona, and Nevada; some of them were also known as Chemehuevis. The two groups spoke different Shoshonean languages.

They sheltered themselves in small dwellings called wickiups. The dwellings were cone shaped and made of sagebrush or reeds. Because the regions in which the Paiutes lived had so little rainfall, a top to the cone was not necessary.

In the early years of European contact in North America, the Sierra Nevada Mountain range on the west and the Wasatch range of the Rocky Mountains to the east shielded the Paiutes from frequent visits by non-Indians. The Paiutes only rarely had to defend themselves and were primarily concerned with finding enough food and water

Eunice Surveyor, a Utah Paiute, working at Paiute Fabrics, a Paiute tribal business in Cedar City, Utah.

to survive each year. At times, Euro-Americans would band together into shooting parties and kill the Paiutes for target practice. If the Paiutes got word that these people were coming, they ran for cover, often hiding their children by burying them in the sand up to their necks and then placing brush around the children's heads.

By the 1860s, the railroad had come through the Great Basin, disturbing the Paiutes' way of life. About the same time, ranchers appeared on the lands. The United States government took over the Great Basin in 1863, and the Paiutes were put on reservations. Their lands were taken from them without payment or treaty.

The tribe did not have a formal centralized government. When there were important issues to discuss, an elder would take charge. To heal their ailments, the Paiutes traditionally turned to a medicine person, man or woman. The healer's power came from animal spirits—the antelope, bear, eagle, mountain goat, owl, and snake—that would appear in dreams. The Paiutes believed that illness occurred when the soul was stolen or lost. They also believed that all material things should be shared and felt they must give back to the earth in equal amounts according to what they took. According to the Paiutes, many things in everyday life, including the eagle, were sacred, and they created and sang songs about their dreams.

In 1889, a Paiute from Nevada named Wovoka (also known as Jack Wilson) experienced a vision that brought about the Ghost Dance religion. The religion spread from the Paiutes to many other tribes. From his revelation, Wovoka preached the end of the earth as it was known and the coming of an Indian Messiah who would make the European-Americans disappear, restore the earth, and bring back Indians and buffalo killed by white settlers and soldiers. The lands would once again belong to the Indian people; disease, starvation, and war would be ended. Wovoka said that he was instructed that Indians must rid themselves of the white man's ways, especially the consumption of alcohol, and learn to live together in peace.

Wovoka also preached meditation and chanting, and he taught other Indians to perform the dance that would bring the Messiah to them more quickly. The dance was called the Ghost Dance by non-Indians because the ghosts of dead Indians were said to be present at the ceremonies. As the Ghost Dance quickly spread among other Indian nations in the West, it also struck fear into the leaders of the U.S. government, and they moved in to stop it. These attempts to halt the Ghost Dance resulted in the massacre of hundreds of Sioux and Cheyennes at Wounded Knee in 1890.

Today, Paiutes live on- and off-reservation throughout the West, particularly in the states of Arizona, California, Nevada, Oregon, and Utah. Many Paiutes make their living working on farms and ranches.

— B. J. Behm

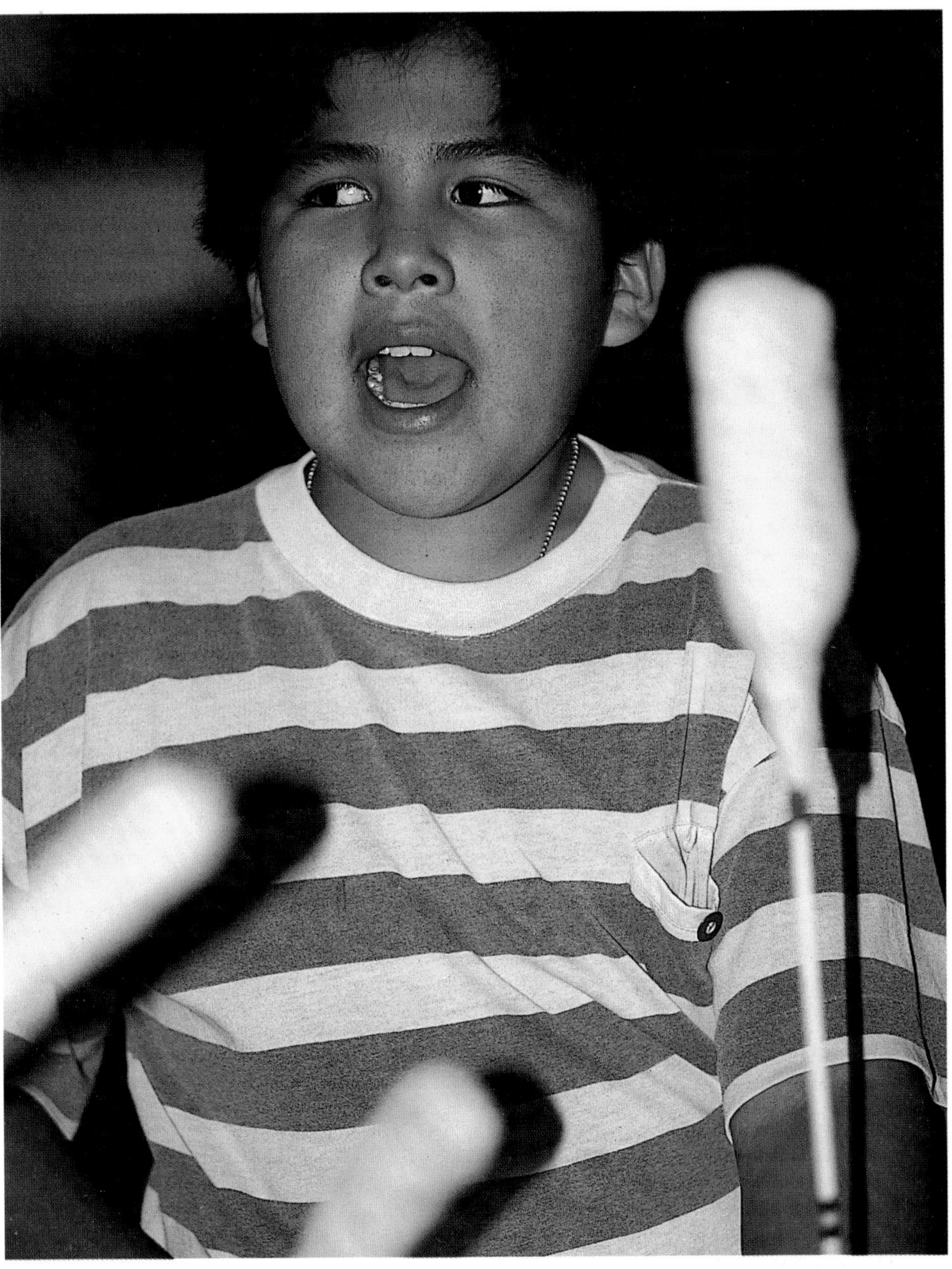

A boy from the Moapa band of Paiutes at drum practice in Moapa, Nevada.

SEE ALSO:
Ghost Dance Religion; Wounded Knee (1890); Wovoka.

SUGGESTED READINGS:

Forbes, Jack D. *Nevada Indians Speak.* Reno: University of Nevada Press, 1967.

Hirschfelder, Arlene, and Martha Kreipe de Montaño. *The Native American Almanac: A Portrait of Native America Today.* New York: Prentice Hall General Reference, 1993.

Waldman, Carl. *Atlas of the North American Indian.* New York: Facts On File, 1985.

PAN-INDIAN (INTERTRIBAL) MOVEMENTS

Before contact with Europeans, most Native Americans referred to their own tribal or national group as "the people." Generally, they had no idea of a common continent-wide ethnicity until European immigrants cast them in common as "Indians." Following contact, however, Native Americans have often used the idea of a common ethnicity

A news photo of American Indians demonstrating in front of the Bureau of Indian Affairs in Washington, D.C., in 1972. Indians from a wide variety of cultures and locales have united in their opposition to government policies against Native peoples.

to organize politically and to socialize. Each type of organization has been an attempt to preserve Native land, resources, and cultures. In our own time, Native Americans have had many national organizations along professional lines as well; tribes with energy resources are organized, as are Native Americans who are journalists, engineers, scientists, and literary writers. In addition to these associations, Indian people meet at powwows, conferences, runs and walks, and other intertribal gatherings that foster a unity of purpose and identity while preserving the unique cultural characteristics of the various assembled groups.

In the colonial period, many pan-Native alliances were formed, as in the Pueblo and Great Southwestern revolts of 1680 and 1698 and the 1675–1676 New England resistance led by King Philip (Metacom), which came to be called King Philip's War. Later, Shawnee groups were especially active in organizing pan-Native resistance to the English from South Carolina northward, while Mahikani (Mahican) people were active in the Ohio country.

In Mexico and elsewhere in present-day Latin America, there were huge Native rebellions, such as the Mixtec War in Mexico and rebellions in the Andean region of South America.

Early in the political history of the United States, some Native American leaders sought to build pan-Indian defenses against the westward expansion of European-Americans. The most famous of these chiefs was Tecumseh, but Pontiac, Neolin the prophet, and others tried to unify many Indian nations.

One of the most effective responses to the severe repression of Native peoples and cultures at the end of the nineteenth century was religious. After the Ghost Dance (a pan-Indian religious movement) played a role in the massacre at Wounded Knee in 1890, most practice of Native religions went underground. The Native American Church is historically important not only because it preserved Native culture underground (and therefore revived forms of community that were being lost to assimilation), but also because it was an early example of a successful pan-Indian movement.

Like the religion begun by the Iroquois Handsome Lake a century earlier, the Native American Church sought Native members only (although a few African-Americans attended peyote meetings in Oklahoma), and it thus sometimes carried the air of a secret society, especially in the eyes of non-Indians. Both religions rejected aspects of European culture that had proved particularly harmful to Native people, especially alcohol. Both religions mixed Native belief and custom with some aspects of Christianity. Both continue to attract adherents today.

In the 1940s, the National Congress of American Indians was formed, composed mostly of wealthy acculturated Indians who were not members of impoverished communities. Their claim to "Indianness" largely rested on blood quantum (percentage of Indian blood) rather than social relationships.

In the political arena, a number of Native American advocacy groups have arisen since the 1960s. Voices of protest were raised at the American Indian Chicago Conference, which brought together more than five hundred Native people from more than sixty groups in 1961. The conference was organized by Sol Tax, professor of anthropology at the University of Chicago, as a forum to enable Native people to express their views regarding their own futures. The National Indian Youth Council (NIYC) organized in the early 1960s.

In 1968, the American Indian Movement (AIM) was formed in Minneapolis to combat police brutality and the selective law enforcement policies of the Minneapolis police. An "Indian patrol" was initially established to follow the police as they traveled through Native American neighborhoods. Within just nine months of the AIM patrols being introduced, arrest rates of Native Americans fell to the general average of the city.

With the assistance of many other Native organizations, AIM organized the siege of Alcatraz Island shortly afterward. With the struggle against termination as a catalyst, pan-Indian activism was transformed by the occupation of this former federal penitentiary at Alcatraz on November 9, 1969. The resulting media attention provided a national platform for discussion of American Indian issues relating to self-determination. The objectives of the occupation included building an American Indian culture center and launching a nationalistic Native American movement called the Confederation of American Indian Nations (CAIN).

On December 16, 1969, the occupants at Alcatraz issued the following statement: "We are issuing this call in an attempt to unify our Indian brothers behind a common cause. . . . We are not getting anywhere fast by working alone as individual tribes. If we can get together as brothers and come to a common agreement, we feel that we can be much more effective, doing things for ourselves, instead of having someone else doing it, telling us what is good for us. So we must start somewhere. We feel that if we are going to succeed, we must hold on to the old ways. *This is the first and most important reason we went to Alcatraz Island.*"

With their focus on pan-Indian unity and identity, the leaders at Alcatraz wanted to create a movement for national American Indian autonomy that would resolve two seemingly competing goals: the goal of unity among various Indian tribes on one hand and, on the other hand, the goal of tribal self-determination (a particular tribe's right to control its own destiny). In reality, the Alcatraz protesters saw some of their goals achieved even though they left the island in 1971. Although the seizure of Alcatraz did not result in gaining title to the island and building an American Indian culture center, it did focus attention, as no one had done before, on the Native American issues of American Indian identity, self-determination, and tribal lands.

AIM and other nationalistic groups created a new sense of independence among young and traditionalist Native Americans. By questioning the validity of tribal governments controlled by the United States government, AIM and the National Indian Youth Council (NIYC) had created an independent alternative leadership. Tribal leaders were criticized as pawns of the Bureau of Indian Affairs (BIA) who were unwilling to protest government policies. AIM leaders also protested Native American educational systems and criticized school programs that demeaned Native Americans. In addition, Dennis Banks and Russell Means of AIM opposed tribal governments established under the Indian Reorganization Act of 1934 because the system fostered corruption and self-interest. Representative government, lobbying, and majority rule were unfamiliar to many traditional tribal governing structures, according to AIM. Hence, AIM advocated a return to consensus building, unanimity, and tribal authority associated with kinship. AIM's leadership role in promoting multitribal unity has been a stormy one that has not always appealed to all Native Americans. And yet, along with various other Indian groups, AIM has given Native people an opportunity to focus on tribal issues as *Indian* issues of concern to all Indian people.

— B. E. Johansen

SEE ALSO:
Alcatraz Island, Occupation of; American Indian Historical Society; American Indian Movement; American Indian Science and Engineering Society; Banks, Dennis; Black Hawk; Council of Energy Resource Tribes; Ghost Dance Religion; Handsome Lake; King Philip's War; Longhouse Religion; Means, Russell; Mixtec; Native American Church; Native American Journalists Association; Pontiac; Powwows; Pueblo Revolt of 1680; Returning the Gift; Shawnee; Tecumseh; Wovoka.

SUGGESTED READINGS:
Dowd, Gregory Evans. *A Spirited Resistance: The North American Indian Struggle for Unity, 1745–1815*. Baltimore: Johns Hopkins University Press, 1991.

Hertzberg, Hazel W. *The Search for an American Indian Identity: Modern Pan-Indian Movements*. Syracuse, NY: Syracuse University Press, 1971.

Nabokov, Peter. *Native American Testimony: A Chronicle of Indian-White Relations from Prophecy to the Present, 1492–1992*. New York: Viking Press, 1992.

PAPAGO

SEE Tohono O'odham.

PAPAL BULL

Throughout the age of European "discovery" of lands in Africa, the Americas, and parts of Asia, European monarchs, clergymen, explorers, soldiers, and settlers used a variety of reasons to justify their conquest of indigenous peoples. Often the exploration and conquest of foreign lands was justified by reason of establishing trade or military might. Just as often, and many times in combination with other reasons, the justification was on religious grounds. As Europeans made increasing contact with indigenous peoples on other continents, they became less and less tolerant of non-Christian cultures. This lack of tolerance became evident in the number of priests and other missionaries who established churches and missions in the midst of indigenous populations. It also became evident in the frequently brutal treatment of non-Christians, who were often looked upon by missionaries and explorers as something less than human.

Then, like today, the Catholic Church issued official doctrines, called papal bulls, in order to further church policies and teachings. In the age when Europeans were making early contact with native populations in other parts of the world, many papal bulls contributed substantially to the way in which Europeans viewed and treated non-Christians. These papal bulls instructed Christians "to capture, vanquish, and subdue" enemies of Christ and to take away all of their property and possessions. In the years since the early exploration of the Americas, these doctrines sometimes became the basis for ongoing patterns of oppression of Indian people, even making their presence felt in the federal laws and other institutions of the United States.

One papal document—a decree issued by Pope Nicholas V in 1452—called upon Portuguese King Alfonso to "invade, search out, capture, vanquish and subdue all . . . pagans . . . and other enemies of Christ." It also states that the land and possessions of these people should be taken away and that non-Christians should be "reduced to perpetual slavery." Another papal bull, the Inter Cetera papal bull, was issued by Pope Alexander VI. It decreed that "barbarous" nations be overthrown and that those nations "discovered" should be conquered and converted to the Catholic faith to propagate Christianity.

Today, many Native people believe that these doctrines set the stage for five hundred years of warfare against Native peoples and made it virtually impossible for the Christian world to respect Native nations in the Western Hemisphere. For example, the land Christopher Columbus took into possession was thought to belong to nobody because the lands were not the property of Christians.

Some of these doctrines have served as the foundation of federal Indian policy that denies Indians their rights to ancestral homelands because they were not Christian. The doctrines have also been incorporated into Supreme Court decisions that distinguish between Christians and "heathens"—that is, those who do not believe in the Christian god. This term would have thus related to almost all Native American peoples from colonial times through the early history of the United States as an independent nation.

Although the distinctions between Christians and non-Christians may not apply in the same way as they did in the early days of the republic, the Supreme Court's distinction between Christians and heathens has found its way into the various laws by which the government regards Native peoples. Under federal law, for example, the United States still denies Indian people their rights to their ancestral homes, and in many respects, they still are not recognized by the government as sovereign nations.

Many Native people today feel that the Church is still in a position to influence non-Indian Americans' views of Native people and their spirituality. In recent years, Native Americans have asked Pope John Paul II to revoke the Inter Cetera papal bull. These people feel that such an act would show support for Native peoples and help communicate to non-Indians the indigenous principle of respect for the earth as the Mother of all people and the respect for all living things that grow out of the earth.

— S. S. Davis

SEE ALSO:
Catholic Church in the Spanish Empire; Christian Colonists' Views of Natives; Missions for Indians, Christian.

PARFLECHE

From the French *parer* and *fleche*, meaning to ward off arrows, *parfleche* was the term given to describe the stiff rawhide shields used by Plains warriors. The term became generic for all items of rawhide, including painted containers.

An assortment of parfleche items distinguished by their geometric designs and bold colors. All of these items are rawhide, and they are all of Sioux origin, with the exception of the envelope at the top of the picture, which is Nez Perce.

bounties, frequently went among them only to enrich himself in the shortest possible time, at the cost of the Indians, and spend the largest available sum of the government money with the least ostensible beneficial result."

During his later years, Parker made a large amount of money playing the stock market but was ruined when he was forced to pay the bond of another man who had defaulted. After retiring from service with the United States government, Parker was appointed New York City building superintendent in 1876. He held the post until he died in 1905. Parker was buried in Buffalo, New York, in a common plot with his grandfather Red Jacket.

— B. E. Johansen

SEE ALSO:
Civil War, U.S., Indians in the; Grant, Ulysses S.; Iroquois Confederacy; Red Jacket.

PARKER, QUANAH (1852–1911)

Comanche leader Quanah Parker, born in Cedar Lake, Texas, in 1852, was a remarkable figure in American history. Parker was an influential negotiator with government agents, a successful cattle rancher and businessman, an activist for Native American education, and a devoted member of the Native American Church.

Parker was born to Peta Nocona, a Quahadi Comanche war chief, and Cynthia Ann Parker, a white woman who had been captured by the Comanches during the Fort Parker raid in Texas on May 19, 1836. Cynthia Ann Parker was renamed Preloch and raised in a traditional Quahadi village, where she eventually married Peta Nocona. In 1861, Cynthia was recaptured by Texas Rangers, leaving young Quanah bereft. Parker's father, Peta Nocona, died in 1866.

In 1867, the Treaty of Medicine Lodge was signed, which established settlements of the Comanches, Cheyennes, Kiowa-Apaches, and Arapahos on reservations in Indian Territory (present-day Oklahoma). A large number of Comanches were agreeable to the treaty's terms, but the Quahadi Comanches resisted for seven years, retaliating with raids and open hostility toward settlers. Foremost among the grievances of the Quahadi was the increasing presence of hired buffalo hunters who threatened to wipe out vast populations of buffalo; this would force Indians onto reservations to avoid starvation. In June of 1875, some seven hundred warriors, including Quanah Parker, attacked a group of buffalo hunters at Adobe Walls in the Texas Panhandle, leading to three days of fighting before the Indians were forced to retreat. In the same year, the Quahadi surrendered to reservation settlement.

In the next several years, Parker's leadership status among his people grew, and he eventually became a member of the Comanche Council. The Comanche Council opposed the Indian department's decision to consolidate the Wichita, Kiowa, Kiowa-Apache, and Comanche agencies and move the headquarters from Fort Sill, Oklahoma, to the Washita River. This move would place the source of rations sixty miles (ninety-seven kilometers) away from the Comanche settlements. Quanah Parker, as a member of the council, joined in the opposition.

In the early 1880s, cattlemen across Texas were driving their herds through Comanche territory. At first, the Comanches tolerated the trespassing, just as the cattlemen ignored the occasional poaching of a cow by the Indians. Opposition from the Comanches eventually arose, however, when ranchers in the areas adjoining Comanche land began ranging their cattle on the grasslands belonging to the Comanches. In 1881, the Comanche Council approved motions to protest the trespassing. Parker, along with two other Comanches, Eschiti and Permansu, was placed on the cattlemen's payroll and hired to ride with the white "cattle police" to monitor the property lines. This was the beginning of Parker's career as a cattle rancher. With the money he made from the cattlemen, he started his own herd and eventually built a ranch named Star House.

In 1884, Parker made his first of twenty trips to Washington, D.C. This trip was to deal with alterations in the lease arrangements the Comanches had secured with the cattlemen. The Comanches were leasing grasslands to the ranchers; however, much of the Comanche land was being divided up through the process of land allotment by the government. (Under the General Allotment Act, tribal lands were being divided up and made available first to individual Indians for ownership and then for settlement by non-Indians.) Parker made several trips to Washington but was not able to stave off the allotment of Comanche land. However, thanks in part to his understanding of how to negotiate with European-Americans and of the laws concerning land and landownership, Parker was able to make deals with white investors that benefited the Comanches.

An undated photo of Quanah Parker, a skilled Comanche leader, businessman, and negotiator.

Quanah Parker was thought to be a "controversial" figure by members of the Indian agency. Many were appalled that Parker was a strong believer in polygamy and carried the distinction of a "road man" (a ritual leader) of the Comanche branch of the Peyote cult. Parker was also suspect among the more traditional members of the Comanche Nation. Though he remained very influential among his people, some of his actions were highly criticized. For instance, in the 1890s, when the Indian agent was issuing formal "chief certificates," Parker convinced the agency that he should be issued the certificate for the principal chieftainship. Many Comanches viewed Parker as the source of their problems—that Parker was a "white man's Indian"—because of his association with U.S. presidents and British lords.

In the first decade of the twentieth century, Parker's influence within tribal politics began to diminish. He lost much of his land and personal fortune because of allotment, and eventually he was forced to take a position with the Indian service as an "assistant farmer." On February 25, 1911, Parker died at the Star House from heart problems.

— T. Midge

See also:
Cheyenne; Comanche; General Allotment Act; Kiowa; Kiowa-Apache; Native American Church.

PASSAMAQUODDY

The Passamaquoddy are historically an Algonquian-speaking tribe that was part of the Abenaki Confederacy. Like other New England Algonquian groups, the Passamaquoddy depended heavily on the numerous New England rivers, lakes, and bays for a living. In fact, their name is derived from the term *those who pursue the pollack,* a fish common to their region.

In 1790, Congress passed the Indian Trade and Intercourse Act; one of its provisions was that Congress approve any land transactions between Indians and non-Indians before the transaction was considered valid. Nearly two hundred years later, in the 1970s, the Penobscot and Passamaquoddy tribes offered proof of a valid claim to most of the state of Maine, citing that act. Their award, including money and land, is one of the greatest Native American land-rights victories of the late twentieth century.

In 1957, documents were discovered indicating that a treaty signed during 1794 between the Passamaquoddy and officials of Massachusetts had never been approved by Congress. The treaty, which ceded much of Maine, was not valid.

In 1980, the Passamaquoddy and Penobscot tribes were each awarded $40.3 million to settle legal claims to about two-thirds of the state of Maine, or 12 million acres (4.8 million hectares). Instead of distributing money to each tribal member in per capita payments, the tribes decided to invest the money in land and business ventures to reestablish a tribal identity. Before the land-claims settlement, the Passamaquoddy had inhabited a small and shrinking reservation; at one point, U.S. Route 1 was built through the reservation, and non-Indian families moved in without asking permission or paying for the land.

The Passamaquoddy began to fight back in the 1960s. By 1975, a federal court had ruled that federal trust responsibility applied to the Passamaquoddy, meaning that the U.S. Justice Department was now obliged to sue the state of Maine on the Passamaquoddy's behalf. In Maine, where the state capitol at Augusta was built in 1832 with money from the sale of Indian land taken under the 1794 treaty, attorneys prepared their case on grounds that the tribe's 180-year-old claim had legally expired. When federal courts held that treaty claims don't simply expire, the state settled out of court.

One-third of the Passamaquoddy's settlement money was spent on 300,000 acres (120,000 hectares) of land. One-third was placed in conservative financial investments; the interest and dividends of these investments were earmarked for payments to tribal members each year. The remaining third was invested in business ventures under a tribal management firm, Tribal Assets Management.

The two tribes suddenly found themselves holding the largest pool of investment capital in Maine. The Passamaquoddy invested a large portion of their capital in one of Maine's largest blueberry farms. The farm was so profitable that the tribe recovered its investment in two years. In 1983, the Passamaquoddy bought the only cement plant in New England. They sold the plant five years later at a profit of $60 million. With the Penobscots, the Passamaquoddy tribes send a nonvoting delegate to the Maine state legislature.

See also:
Abenaki; Indian Trade and Intercourse Acts; Maine; Penobscot.

PAWNEE

While the Pawnees called themselves Chahiksichahiks, or "Men of Men," they are best known from the Choctaw term used to describe a curve or twist. This may have referred to the way the Pawnees wore their hair in a scalp lock stiffened with red ocher and buffalo fat until it stood up and curved backward like a horn. Their name may also be related to *Pani,* a term used by the French for certain Caddoan tribes once living in the area of Oklahoma, as well as for the Pawnees of today.

The Pawnees were originally from the lower Mississippi Valley or the area of present-day Oklahoma and are closely related to the Arikara and the Wichita Nations. Their villages consisted of earth-covered lodges built along the Platte and Republican Rivers. By 1702, two thousand Pawnee families were living in the central Plains area. They fought the Sioux and Cheyennes and raided the Comanches to obtain horses. They were also avid traders.

Historically, the Pawnees have been described as a nation with a religion that is rich in myth, symbolism, and poetic fancy. They performed elaborate rites and ceremonies connected with the stars and other heavenly bodies. Pawnees believe in one deity, the creator of all things. Their religious beliefs were integrated with almost all of their practices, including war parties and buffalo hunts. This developed strong personal characteristics among the Pawnees, known for their courage, loyalty, and respect for authority. Historians have also noted their endurance and energy. In the late nineteenth century, they continued the Ghost Dance, using this religious ceremony to contact dead medicine men and, through them, to recreate religious rituals that had been lost.

A Pawnee community as it appeared to early European settlers, crowded with earth-covered dwellings.

The Pawnees made early European contact with Spanish explorers in the 1500s. Three centuries later, the United States claimed Pawnee territory through the Louisiana Purchase of 1803. St. Louis became a major trading center for the Pawnees after the purchase. With European-American settler immigration to the west, Pawnee land was traveled frequently. Because of this exposure to European-Americans and their diseases, the nation was almost destroyed through epidemics.

The Pawnees were removed from their lands through three treaties in the mid-1800s. Through the treaties they were offered a reservation in Nebraska, where they were constantly raided by the Sioux (Dakota, Lakota, and Nakota) Nations. This and other difficulties caused the Pawnees to consider moving to Indian Territory in present-day Oklahoma. They went south, surveyed the land, and finally ceded their Nebraska reservation for one in Indian Territory. A tract of land between the Arkansas and Cimarron Rivers was selected. The purchase of the 283,020-acre (113,208-hectare) reservation from their own tribal funds was confirmed by Congress in 1876. There, the Pawnees immediately built a new tribal agency, homes, shops, schools, and stables, and their descendants occupy this area, near the town of Pawnee, Oklahoma, today.

Pawnees were often used as scouts for the United States government in its campaign against other Indian nations. Following a practice that Euro-Americans had developed in their relations with Native peoples since colonial days, the United States was able to exploit Native people's skills, their ability to understand the motives and ways of other Native peoples and old tribal enmities, in a campaign to divide and conquer. After the death of General George Armstrong Custer, the United States Army enlisted one hundred Pawnees for a military campaign against the Sioux.

On the Oklahoma reservation, the Pawnees raised livestock, but income from this was low. They opened up their lands to lease for grazing, and that brought in a small revenue for the nation. Most of their reservation was rough, with rocky hills, ravines, and scrub timber. And raising crops on the reservation was difficult, to say the least.

Since their struggle for mere survival was difficult, the United States was able to reach an easy agreement for the cession of the Pawnee land and for individual allotments. Their land was opened up for settlement with the Oklahoma Land Run of 1893. By 1906, diseases brought by the settlers had decimated the tribe to 649 individuals.

The Pawnees reorganized under the Oklahoma Indian Welfare Act of 1936 as the Pawnee Indian Tribe of Oklahoma with a constitution and bylaws. They were issued a charter by the Department of the Interior, and it was ratified by the Pawnee Nation in an election on April 28, 1938.

— S. S. Davis

SEE ALSO:
Caddo; Epidemic Diseases; General Allotment Act; Oklahoma.

PEA RIDGE, BATTLE OF

Also known as the Battle of Elkhorn Tavern, this engagement of the U.S. Civil War took place in Benton County, Arkansas, on March 7 and 8, 1862. The battle secured Union control of Missouri and was one of the few major battles fought west of the Mississippi River.

The battle also has significance in U.S. history because of the participation of Native American troops from Indian Territory (present-day Oklahoma) on the side of the Confederacy. At the outset of the Civil War, Albert Pike, an Arkansas politician, negotiated treaties between the Confederacy and the so-called Five Civilized Tribes (Cherokee, Chickasaw, Choctaw, Creek, and Seminole), which had been removed to Indian Territory from their homelands in the Southeast. As part of the treaties, the tribes were permitted to organize home guard units to protect Indian Territory from possible Union invasion from Kansas. Thus created were the 1st Regiment Choctaw and Chickasaw Mounted Rifles under Colonel Douglas H. Cooper, the 1st Creek Regiment under Colonel D. N. McIntosh, the 1st Regiment Cherokee Mounted Rifles under Colonel John Drew, and the 2nd Regiment Cherokee Mounted Rifles under Colonel Stand Watie.

Major General Earl Van Dorn took command of the Trans-Mississippi District for the Confederacy in January of 1862. His objective was to protect Arkansas and provide relief for Confederate supporters in Missouri. He intended to achieve this by capturing St. Louis. Van Dorn's armies gathered near Fayetteville, Arkansas. In addition to troops from Missouri, Arkansas, Texas, and Louisiana, Van Dorn summoned Albert Pike and his Indian home guard from Indian Territory. According to the treaties, the Indian troops were not permitted to serve outside of Indian Territory without their consent, but Van Dorn chose to ignore the treaties and ordered the Native American troops to prepare for the invasion of Missouri.

The Union forces in Missouri were commanded by Brigadier General Samuel Curtis, whose objective was to secure Missouri from the Confederates and if possible to push them farther south. Curtis's force of 10,250 and Van Dorn's force of 17,000 (including 2,500 Indian troops under the command of Pike) met in the northwest corner of Arkansas at Elkhorn Tavern. The troops skirmished on March 6 and met in battle on March 7 and 8. The Confederates split forces in an attempt to outflank the Union troops, but when several key Confederate officers were killed, large numbers of troops were left leaderless and in disarray. The Confederate armies consolidated on March 8, only to find that they were low on ammunition. Retreat was inevitable.

The Native troops under Pike fared as well as any of the regular Confederate forces. There were reports that the Native troops had reverted to their old ways of fighting, similar to guerrilla warfare, but in fact they were not trained to fight any other way.

There were accusations of battlefield atrocities, including scalping, against the Native American troops, but there were also reports of heroism. In what could be considered one of the few Confederate successes of the battle, Colonel Stand Watie and his Cherokee Mounted Rifles managed to overcome a Union Artillery battery and help secure an orderly retreat of Confederate forces. This was the first and last time that Indian forces participated in the U.S. Civil War on any large scale.

SEE ALSO:
Cherokee; Chickasaw; Choctaw; Civil War, U.S., Indians in the; Creek; Five Civilized Tribes; Oklahoma; Seminole; Watie, Stand.

PELTIER, LEONARD
(1944–)

Leonard Peltier was born on September 12, 1944, in Grand Forks, North Dakota. He is an Ojibwe-Sioux from the Turtle Mountain Reservation. A boarding-school student as a young child, Peltier became actively involved as a teenager in trying to stop the termination of his nation by helping his father on a petition drive. At the age of twenty, Peltier co-owned an auto body shop in Seattle, Washington; above the auto shop, he provided a place for Indians who were down on their luck and trying to find jobs within the community.

Leonard Peltier, as photographed in prison in 1991. Peltier continues to maintain his innocence in the killings of two FBI agents, for which he was convicted and sentenced to two consecutive life terms at Fort Leavenworth Penitentiary in 1976. His case continues to receive international attention.

Peltier's first experience with the American Indian Movement (AIM) was in 1970 at the Fort Lawton takeover outside Seattle. He then traveled around New Mexico and Arizona, working on Navajo civil-rights violations. In Denver, he met with Vernon Bellecourt, who explained what AIM was trying to do and took Peltier to an AIM meeting.

Peltier became a central figure in AIM, going on the Trail of Broken Treaties, which dramatized a variety of grievances against the U.S. government's policies and treatment of Native people, and participating in the occupation of Wounded Knee (the site of a massacre of hundreds of Indians by U.S. troops in 1890), a small town on the Pine Ridge Reservation in South Dakota. As part of the security force of AIM, Peltier and others of Northwest AIM were called to set up camp and protect the people of the reservation during a time of turmoil and confrontation between Indians and the government. The group was camped at the Jumping Bull ranch, along with several women and children.

These demonstrators at a rally calling for an inquiry into the case against Leonard Peltier are among a large number of people who feel that his murder convictions were based on questionable evidence and testimony.

On June 26, 1975, two FBI agents followed a red pickup truck onto the Jumping Bull compound (which consisted of a couple of houses), and a firefight followed between members of AIM and the agents. The agents were reportedly searching for a man who had stolen a pair of cowboy boots. During the firefight, the two agents were shot at close range and killed. Soon afterward, the compound was surrounded by federal agents, and subsequently a young Indian man was shot and killed.

The seventeen or more people at the compound managed to escape, and the ensuing manhunt for the murderer of the agents was the biggest in FBI history. Peltier was indicted for this murder, as was his cousin Robert Robideau and fellow AIM member Darrelle (Dino) Butler. Peltier went to Canada and fought extradition, while Robideau and Butler were sent to court and were acquitted on grounds of self-defense. Using affidavits concerning Peltier's involvement in the firefight submitted by a woman who later admitted that she had been coerced by agents into making false statements, the FBI was able to extradite Peltier and put him on trial in Fargo, North Dakota.

Peltier's trial was riddled with coerced testimony, and the prosecution withheld evidence that would have helped him in the case. The lead prosecutor in the case, Lynn Crooks, has said that he does not know who killed the agents. Even so, Peltier was convicted of murdering the agents and sent to prison to serve two consecutive life sentences. In prison, his life has been threatened by people who claim the FBI put them up to it.

Peltier has been in prison since 1976 and still maintains he is innocent. He has appealed his case several times, but the court has refused to rehear his case. Only in the 1980s, through the Freedom of Information Act, were some of the odd circumstances surrounding his trial and case revealed. In the 1990s, a man known only as Mr. X came forward (without revealing his identity) and claimed he was the man who killed the agents.

Peltier has support from people worldwide who want his case reviewed and would like to see him free. United States senators and representatives, Nobel Peace Prize recipients, and numerous others who are internationally known have asked the United States government to review the case or grant executive clemency to Peltier. As of 1996, this has not happened.

Peltier has a national-international defense committee in Lawrence, Kansas, whose mission is to inform more people about his case and thus generate more popular support. He is currently serving his sentence in Leavenworth Federal Penitentiary in Kansas.

— S. S. Davis

SEE ALSO:
American Indian Movement; Bellecourt, Clyde and Vernon; Boarding Schools; Butler, Darrelle; Robideau, Robert; Termination Policy; Trail of Broken Treaties; Wounded Knee (1890); Wounded Knee, Confrontation at (1973).

PENNSYLVANIA

Pennsylvania, which became the second U.S. state on December 12, 1787, is named for Admiral William Penn, the father of the founder of the Pennsylvania colony. Pennsylvania has a long history of Native peoples living in the area. The Meadowcroft Rockshelter site, where Indians once lived, has been dated as being over twelve thousand years old. There is also a great deal of evidence of Eastern Woodland sites in the region that date back over one thousand years.

In the early 1600s, Dutch and Swedish explorers visited parts of eastern Pennsylvania. In 1643, Swedish settlers established the first permanent European settlements in Pennsylvania at Tinicum and New Gottenburg. The Dutch took control of the region from the Swedish in 1655, but they lost their colonies in Pennsylvania and in New York to the English in 1664. In 1681, William Penn (Admiral Penn's son) received a grant from Charles II, the King of England, to establish the Providence of Pennsylvania.

Penn's colony was governed by laws that allowed for a great deal of personal freedom. Penn also differed from other English colonial leaders in his dealings with Indians. When Penn established his colony, there were four major Indian groups who lived in the area. These groups were the Lenapes (Delawares), the Shawnees, the Susquehannas, and some members of the Iroquois Confederacy. Penn signed peace treaties with each of these indigenous peoples; and—perhaps more important, when one considers that in future years Euro-Americans would ignore dozens of treaty obligations to American Indians—he honored the treaties that he signed.

Pennsylvania enjoyed a period of peaceful relations between colonists and Indians that lasted for nearly seventy years. In the mid-1700s, pressure from European settlement finally caused a breakdown in the peaceful relationship, and war broke out. The warfare and continued pressure from colonists forced many of the Pennsylvania Indians to move westward into Ohio, and by the late 1700s, few Indians remained in the area.

No Indian reservations currently exist in Pennsylvania. The 1990 U.S. Census lists 14,733 state residents as being American Indians, which ranks Pennsylvania twenty-eighth among states in Native American population.

SEE ALSO:
Iroquois Confederacy; Lenape; Penn, William; Quakers; Shawnee.

PENN, WILLIAM (1644–1718)

Born in England, William Penn became an English Quaker advocate of religious freedom who oversaw the creation of the British colony in North America that came to be known as Pennsylvania. Although most of his life was spent in England, Penn visited North America twice for several years and formed close friendships with several American Indians, notably leaders of the Lenape (Delaware) tribe. The Delaware chief Tammany (or Tammanend) played a prominent role in the early treaties negotiated with Penn.

Even before coming to America, William Penn wrote a letter to the Iroquois reinforcing Quaker and Iroquois ideas of "peace and justice that we may live friendly together as becomes the workmanship of the great God." In 1683, Penn commented in his letter to the Society of Free Traders on the Indians he knew: "Every king hath his council, and that consists of all the old and wise men of his nation . . . nothing is undertaken, be it war, peace, the selling of land or traffick, without advising with them; and which is more, with the young

This painting by Benjamin West is one of the best-known representations of the treaty between William Penn (in black hat with arms outstretched) and American Indians.

men also. . . . The kings . . . move by the breath of their people. . . . It is the Indian custom to deliberate. . . . I have never seen more natural sagacity."

Penn described the Native confederacies of eastern North America as political societies with sachemships, or leadership roles, inherited through the female line. In addition to the above description of tribal councils, Penn briefly described some aspects of the Iroquois Condolence Council. He noted that when someone kills a "woman they pay double" the wampum since ". . . she breeds children which men cannot." While in Pennsylvania, Penn "made himself endeared to the Indians," and he "walked with them, sat with them on the ground, and ate . . . their roasted acorns and homony [sic]."

SEE ALSO:
Iroquois Confederacy; Lenape; Pennsylvania; Tammany.

PENOBSCOT

The Penobscots have lived in the area now known as Maine for centuries. The Penobscot language is of the Algonquian language group, and the tribe is closely related to the Abenaki and Passamaquoddy Nations. During the colonial era, the Penobscots, like the Passamaquoddy and other confederated Abenaki tribes, found themselves drawn into many European conflicts, including those known as the French and Indian War.

European-American settlers were slow to enter Penobscot territory. Following the English colonization of Massachusetts, the Penobscots presented a formidable obstacle to the English advance. Madokawando (c. 1630–1698), a Penobscot sachem in the Abenaki Confederacy, was initially neutral in the British struggle with France in North America. But later, he allied with the French through

A photo of a Penobscot man taken in Maine in 1925. In 1980, his descendants would win a huge land-rights case against the state.

the marriage of one of his daughters to the Frenchman Jean Vincent de l'Abadie (Baron de St. Castin), who founded a trading post at Castine, Maine. Madokawando also was angered at the spread of English settlement onto Penobscot lands. After British troops plundered the trading post, Madokawando joined the French cause. He and his supporters raided several British settlements, including York, Maine, where they killed seventy-seven people in 1691. For a short time, most settlers were driven out of Maine by these raids.

Madokawando was respected as an enemy because he was humane. In 1689, during the siege of Pemaquid, he was responsible for sparing the lives of Lieutenant James Weems and six other soldiers. By 1693, he realized that, despite his distaste for the English, they would eventually overwhelm the French, so he negotiated a peace at Pemaquid as other chiefs continued to raid English settlements. Madokawando's decision also was influenced by Boston's growing appetite for furs, so he sought peace over the objections of the French and younger Penobscot warriors.

Moxus, one of the most influential leaders among the Penobscots in the late seventeenth and early eighteenth centuries, led some of the most destructive raids on the northern frontiers of early New England. In 1689, he and the Baron de St. Castin routed English settlers at Pemaquid, Maine, capturing several dozen colonists. In July 1694, Moxus, his warriors, and their French allies killed more than one hundred English colonists in the battle of Oyster River, near the site of present-day Durham. Several other deadly raids on a smaller scale followed. Between raids, Moxus professed a desire for peace, as he signed various (usually ineffectual) treaties with various New England officials in 1689, 1699, 1702, 1713, and 1717.

Late in the 1700s, the Penobscots ceded most of their land through treaties and a land sale in 1833. With the loss of their land, the Penobscots ceased to have federal recognition as a nation. During the 1970s, however, discovery of valid land claims enabled the rebuilding of a Penobscot Nation land base.

In the 1970s, under the federal Indian Trade and Intercourse Act of 1790, the Penobscot and Passamaquoddy tribes offered proof of a valid claim to most of the state of Maine. Their award, including money and land, is one of the greatest Native American land-rights victories of the late twentieth century. While the Passamaquoddy investments proved very profitable, those of the Penobscots did not perform as well. The Penobscots built an ice-hockey arena on their reservation, which ran at a loss. A business set up to make audio- and video-cassettes also floundered financially. The Penobscot reservation is at Indian Island, near Old Town, Maine, on the Penobscot River. As with the Passamaquoddy tribe, the Penobscots send a nonvoting delegate to the Maine state legislature.

SEE ALSO:
French and Indian War; Indian Trade and Intercourse Act; Maine; Passamaquoddy.

PENSONEAU, DAVID (1959–)

David Pensoneau, a member of the Ponca Nation, is a United States Chess Federation (USCF) National Master and was Oklahoma Chess Champion in 1984. He is from a large family, the youngest of seven children. All of his brothers and sisters attended Chilocco Indian Agricultural School near their home in Ponca City, Oklahoma. Several of them then attended the University of Oklahoma, and his oldest brother was educated at Harvard and the University of California-Los Angeles. But Chilocco had closed by the time David started school, so he attended the public schools in Ponca City and nearby Tonkawa. He then studied accounting at the University of Oklahoma and at the University of Central Oklahoma.

Pensoneau did not take up chess until he was fourteen, in 1973, when his father gave him a chess book, *Bobby Fischer Teaches Chess*, for a present. He spent about a year studying chess books and playing against relatives before entering his first tournament, a formal competition sponsored by the USCF in Arkansas City, Kansas. To the surprise of the experienced tournament players, he won first place, with two wins and a draw in his three games.

Chess became his passion. Within six months, he had played the required number of tournament games (sixteen) to become a USCF-rated player. His first rating, 1495, like the result of his first tournament, was exceptionally strong. Most USCF players earn a first rating nearer, or below, 1000. To become a USCF Master requires a rating of 2200 or above. Pensoneau set his sights on earning a master's certificate, a distinction that very few tournament chess players achieve.

By the time he graduated from high school in 1977, his rating had climbed to the 1800 to 1850 range. He postponed college to devote his time to chess. In 1978, he played more than one hundred rated tournament games, and his rating climbed steadily into the 1850 to 1900 range. Then he hit a plateau where he couldn't seem to make any headway. He was especially frustrated at not being able to defeat an Expert (USCF Experts are rated just below Masters, at 2000 to 2199).

Pensoneau took a break from the rigors of tournament play for about a year and a half, devoting himself to an intense study of the game. When he returned, he quickly scored his first victory over an Expert, and his own rating climbed steadily, soon topping 2000 as he became a USCF Expert himself. More hard-fought tournament victories pushed his rating to 2150. When he entered the 1984 Oklahoma Championship Tournament, he was unstoppable, emerging as Oklahoma Champion, with a new rating of 2198, just two points shy of his master's certificate.

The next week, Pensoneau entered the University of Oklahoma and had to wait until the end of the semester before he could play in another tournament. In that tournament, he pushed his rating above 2200 and, as a college freshman, became a U.S. Chess Federation National Master. David Pensoneau has maintained his master's certificate since then and has been active in teaching the game to Native youth.

PEQUOT

One of the first Native American nations to come into contact with English colonists in the area later called New England, the Pequots assembled an alliance of Native peoples in 1636 in an effort to drive Puritan settlers out of the area around Boston. Due in part to the Puritans' Native allies, the attempt failed, and the Pequots were nearly exterminated in the Pequot War of 1636. Late in the twentieth century, the remnants of the Pequot

Nation have been reassembling on a small plot of land in Connecticut with a massive cash infusion supplied by the largest Native American gambling operation in New England.

Historically, the Pequots are an Algonquian-speaking people who, in the early 1600s, numbered about twenty-two hundred people. Most lived in the Thames Valley of present-day Connecticut. Their economy was based on hunting, fishing, and the cultivation of corn.

Facing a growing European-American presence spreading from the Boston area, the Pequots split into two factions. One, opponents of the English colonists, was led by Sassacus. At one point, this faction limited its trade to the Dutch. Another faction, led by Uncas, allied with the colonists, often fighting with the English against dissident Pequots and other Native peoples.

Trouble began in the summer of 1636 with the murder of an English trader on Block Island. Massachusetts sent a punitive expedition that spurred the Pequots to defend their shrinking homeland. Most of the Pequots, perhaps as many as six hundred, died in the burning of their main fort at Mystic, Connecticut. Pequots who escaped the inferno at Mystic separated into small bands and tried to escape, but Puritan soldiers tracked them with the aid of Mohegan and Narragansett allies. Many Pequots were sold into slavery to South Carolina, Barbados, and other British colonies. The Mohegans took their land.

Some who surrendered were sent to live with other tribes, but they were treated with such cruelty that the colonial government resettled the remnants of the Pequot Nation on Mystic River in 1655. The population of the area dwindled to about two hundred by 1980, before a large casino drew economic development to the area and spurred a great number of people to apply for tribal enrollment in 1990.

SEE ALSO:
Connecticut; Massachusetts; Pequot War; Uncas.

PEQUOT WAR

The Pequot War, which pitted a Native alliance against the English and several other Native nations, changed the demographic balance in New England. Before it, the English were only a small minority among several populous Native nations. After the war, they were dominant.

This engraving shows an attack on a Pequot encampment by a group of English colonists in Massachusetts.

This structured interdependency is even used to cement bonds between tribes and has prevented wars. The most famous of all these intertribal social-political alliances is that among the nations of the Iroquois Confederacy. Each of the nations in the confederacy has certain duties to the others. Performing the rituals and fulfilling duties within the confederacy is often called "polishing the chain." Similar relationships existed between many other tribes, and some, like those of the Iroquois Confederacy, continue to this day.

Besides the need for harmony within and between tribes, Native Americans feel the need for harmony between themselves and the rest of nature. This element of Native American philosophy is felt so strongly that it is cannot be distinguished from religion. It holds that human beings are just a small part of nature, and our existence is completely dependent on the totality of nature, wherein we fulfill our role in creation.

This view contrasts with the European-American view that seems to be based on the conquest and exploitation of nature. Europeans set themselves apart from and superior to the rest of creation, using technology to bend the world to suit themselves. From a Native perspective, this is hopelessly arrogant and can lead only to disaster.

Susan Picotte-LaFlesche, as photographed around the time of her graduation from Hampton Institute in 1886.

This picture of Native American philosophy is incomplete, and elements of it may not be true for all tribes. However, the importance of harmony within and between people, families, tribes, and the rest of nature is certainly a key to understanding Native American philosophy.

— L. Hester

SEE ALSO:

Cherokee Harmony Ethic; Family, Role in Native Society; Iroquois Confederacy; Moieties.

SUGGESTED READINGS:

Gill, Sam D. *Native American Religions: An Introduction*. Belmont, CA: Wadsworth, 1982.

Harrod, Howard L. *Renewing the World: Plains Indian Religion and Morality*. Tucson: University of Arizona Press, 1987.

Hirschfelder, Arlene, and Paulette Molin. *Encyclopedia of Native American Religions*. New York: Facts on File, 1992.

Tedlock, Dennis, and Barbara Tedlock, eds. *Teachings from the American Earth: Indian Religion and Philosophy*. New York: Liveright, 1975.

Vecsey, Christopher, ed. *Religion in Native North America*. Moscow, ID: University of Idaho Press, 1990.

PHOENIX, CHEROKEE

SEE *Cherokee Phoenix*.

PICOTTE-LaFLESCHE, SUSAN (1865–1915)

Daughter of the Omaha principal chief Joseph LaFlesche, Susan Picotte-LaFlesche became a government doctor on the Omaha Reservation during a time when cholera, influenza, tuberculosis, and other diseases were reaching epidemic proportions. As a young woman, Susan LaFlesche performed outstandingly at a number of European-American schools. As the first American Indian woman to become a physician, she nearly worked herself to death serving the Omahas as a government physician from 1889 to the end of her life in 1915.

In this 1886 photo, taken at Hampton Institute graduation exercises, Susan LaFlesche (center) and other Native students portray Indians of the past, present, and future declaring "their desire to be civilized."

In 1884, after two and a half years at the Elizabeth Institute for Young Ladies in Elizabeth, New Jersey, LaFlesche enrolled at the Hampton Normal and Agricultural Institute in Hampton, Virginia. This vocational school had been started by General Samuel C. Armstrong to educate freed slaves. A number of Indians also attended, and the school played a role in the designs of Lieutenant Richard Henry Pratt, who started the Carlisle Indian School. LaFlesche graduated from Hampton on May 20, 1886, at the top of her class. Between 1886 and 1889, she attended the Women's Medical College of Pennsylvania on a scholarship raised by her friends, many of whom were non-Indian. She graduated at the top of her class. LaFlesche thus became one of a handful of Native American physicians in the nineteenth century, a handful that includes Charles Eastman and Carlos Montezuma.

In December 1891, LaFlesche wrote that influenza "raged with more violence than during the two preceding years. Some families were rendered helpless by it. . . . Almost every day I was out making visits. . . . Several days the temperature was 15 to 20 degrees below zero [F; (26 to 29 degrees below zero C)], and I had to drive [a horse-drawn buggy] myself." During that winter, she treated more than six hundred patients.

By 1892, the intensity of her work was costing LaFlesche her health. She was beset by a number of debilitating illnesses for the rest of her life, as she ministered to the ever-present ills of the Omahas. At one point, she wearily departed for Washington, D.C., to testify for the Omahas. Because her mission was of such importance to them, the Omaha people had threatened to convey her bodily to Washington.

On the Omaha reservation, LaFlesche waged a tireless campaign against alcoholism, recounting stories of how Indians craving alcohol used their rent money and even pawned their clothes in winter to obtain liquor. She wrote of one Harry Edwards, who, on a winter's night in 1894, "fell from a buggy, was not missed by his drunken companions, and in the morning was found frozen to death." From a medical point of view, LaFlesche believed that alcoholism was at the root of many of the physical, mental, and moral ills facing the Omahas and other American Indians.

In 1894, her health improving, she married Henri Picotte, who was part French and part Sioux; she also began a new medical practice for Indians and non-Indians at Bancroft, Nebraska. She practiced medicine there for the rest of her life, as her own health permitted. After her death on September 18, 1915, the Walthill *Times* added an extra page in its September 24 issue and filled it with warm eulogies to her. Friends recalled that hundreds of people in that area, Native and European-American alike, owed their lives to her care.

The hospital that Susan Picotte-LaFlesche built at Walthill has since been declared a national historic landmark. Since 1988, her memory has been celebrated at an annual festival there.

Bert Cooley, a Pima resident at the Gila River Indian Community in Arizona. Like many other residents of the Gila River Reservation, he makes his living farming.

See also:
Carlisle Indian School; Eastman, Charles; Hampton Institute; Montezuma, Carlos; Omaha.

PIERRE, CHIEF GEORGE (1926–)

Chief George Pierre is an Indian writer who was born in 1926 on the east side of the Cascade Mountains. He is a member of the Okanogan tribe and has held the position of chief of the Colville Confederated Tribes of Washington.

In 1972, Chief Pierre wrote *Autumn's Bounty*. The novel's main character is Alphonse, an old Okanogan chief who is fighting against the termination of his tribe. Alphonse sets out to track and kill a cougar that has killed a young girl. The old chief believes the cougar may be the mate of a female he killed ten years before. During the hunt, Alphonse has to fight rabid coyotes and stave off starvation. After he kills the cougar, the coyotes eat all of the animal, except its head. Some critics have compared this novel with Ernest Hemingway's *The Old Man and the Sea*.

See also:
Colville Confederated Tribes.

PIMA

The Pimas are an O'odham-speaking people of the Uto-Aztecan linguistic family. They are closely related to the Papagos (the Tohono O'odham) and the Nevome and Papaq tribes. Since the early nineteenth century, the Pimas have lived in close association with the Maricopas (the Pipatsjis), a Yuman people.

O'odham-speaking peoples, including the Pimas and Papagos, are increasingly being regarded by archaeologists and ethno-historians as the probable descendants of the great Hohokam tradition in the area now known as southern Arizona. The Hohokam tradition flourished at about the same time as two other great Southwest desert traditions, the Anasazi and the Mogollon, and, like the others, had entered into a decline by the fourteenth century. The Hohokam were skilled agricultural engineers who constructed an elaborate network of irrigation canals in the Gila and Salt River Valleys, in the area of the present city of Phoenix, Arizona.

The Pimas were the proprietors of thriving agricultural communities in the Gila and Salt River Valleys when they were first encountered by Europeans—specifically, by Spaniards—in 1697. During the remainder of the Spanish colonial era, the Pimas came into increasing contact with the Spanish as presidios (forts) and missions were established in southern Arizona. When the region came under the influence of the United States in the mid-nineteenth century at the end of the Mexican-American War, the Pimas experienced severe disruptions of their lives, including the loss of many of their water rights. In the late nineteenth and early twentieth centuries, like Indians throughout the country, they endured the assaults on their culture by the government, which attempted to extinguish their language, religion, and culture by imposing the European-American culture on their children in the government boarding schools.

Despite these assaults, the Pimas have endured as a Native people. They are concentrated today in several communities within their ancient homeland, where they pursue self-sufficiency and self-determination through a variety of tribal enterprises. Two of the largest of these communities are the Gila River Indian Community at Sacaton, Arizona, and the Salt River Pima-Maricopa Indian Community at Scottsdale, Arizona.

The Gila River Indian Community is located about 40 miles (64 kilometers) south of Phoenix, Arizona, and consists of 374,361 acres (149,744 hectares). It was established by Congress on February 28, 1895. Tribal membership is about 11,000 with a population of about 9,500 living on the reservation. Agriculture continues to play an important role in the life of the community, with about 34,000 acres (13,600 hectares) in production by the tribe and by individual tribal members. A tribal enterprise known as The Farms has 16,000 acres (6,400 hectares) in production, with an operating budget of $8 million, and provides employment for more than 400 people, about 150 of them fulltime. Crops include alfalfa, barley, citrus fruits, cotton, grapes, lettuce, melons, and onions. The tribe also has three industrial parks that house a wide range of manufacturing operations. An arts and crafts center includes a museum, restaurant, and gift shop. The tribe operates Firebird International Raceway Park, which features Pro-National Hot Rod Association drag racing. A lake is the site of competitive boat racing, while an outdoor amphitheater frequently hosts big-name entertainers. The HuHuKam Memorial Hospital provides health services.

Established by Congress on June 14, 1879, the Salt River Pima-Maricopa Indian Community consists of 52,600 acres (21,040 hectares) on the eastern edge of the city of Phoenix. Tribal members who reside on the reservation number about five thousand. The present constitution of the tribe was adopted on June 15, 1940. Agriculture continues to be important to this community, with about 12,000 acres (4,800 hectares) in production. The tribe operates a cement plant, a solid waste disposal system that serves several nearby cities, and sand and gravel mines. It operates a library and museum, a restaurant, golf courses, swimming pools, baseball fields, and two theater complexes. The community is also the site of the largest commercial development on Indian land in the nation, a 140-acre (56-hectare) retail complex called The Pavilions.

See also:
Anasazi; Boarding Schools; Hohokam; Mexican-American War; Mogollon Culture; New Spain; Spain; Tohono O'odham.

PINE RIDGE RESERVATION, CONFLICT AT

Factionalism—conflict among people within a group—has been an important force in many Native

American societies, past and present. Historically, ever since Spanish conquistador Hernán Cortés forged alliances with enemies of the Aztecs to defeat them, Europeans and Euro-Americans have used factionalism to divide and conquer Indian people. Often, as in the case of Black Hawk and Keokuk during the nineteenth century, the United States undermined support for rebellious Indian leaders by bestowing official titles and economic benefits on their opponents. As the so-called American frontier closed in the late 1880s and lands inhabited solely by Indians gave way permanently to non-Native settlements, this practice was used by United States Indian Agent James McLaughlin to erode popular support for leaders such as Sitting Bull and Red Cloud.

Late in the twentieth century, factionalism and other forms of tribal conflict continued to plague many Native American peoples. One of recent history's most divisive and deadly examples of tribal factionalism—and the fanning of the flames of tribal conflict by non-Indian outsiders—is that of the Pine Ridge Reservation in South Dakota.

During the 1970s, intratribal political and economic conflicts fueled what may easily be described as a civil war on the Oglala Lakota Nation (Pine Ridge Sioux Indian Reservation). The mostly mixed-blood Oglala tribal leaders—known as assimilationists because they favored working more closely with the government—generally opposed the preserving of traditional governance on the reservation. These tribal leaders were frightened by recent protests that had led to takeovers by Indian people at the Bureau of Indian Affairs (BIA) in Washington, D.C., and in Wounded Knee, South Dakota. Backed by a private police force with further support from the Federal Bureau of Investigation (FBI), the assimilationist leaders tried to repress a growing grassroots movement that promoted tribal self-determination.

Those who favored tribal self-determination were called traditionals because of their support for more traditional forms of tribal governance and greater independence from the U.S. government. Beginning in the late 1960s, the traditionals found a frequent ally in the American Indian Movement (AIM), which had urban roots.

Dick Wilson was first elected chairman of the Pine Ridge Reservation Tribal Council in 1972. Shortly thereafter, traditionals organized the Oglala Sioux Constitutional Rights Organization (OSCRO). Instead of working with the traditionals, Wilson responded by outfitting a personal police force, a group so nakedly brutal that it was called (and members even called themselves) the "goon squad." (To Wilson supporters, the phrase stood for "Guardians of the Oglala Nation.")

One result of the escalating conflict between the traditionals and Wilson was the seventy-one-day occupation of Wounded Knee in 1973. The occupation took place as part of an effort by traditionals to publically confront Wilson's tribal policies, which often wound up favoring non-Indian ranchers, farmers, and corporations. During and after the occupation of Wounded Knee, the FBI steadily became more and more involved in the conflict, siding with the assimilationists. In addition to the traditionals' resentment over being denied responsibility for their own communities, land, and resources (and their resulting impoverishment), a major cause of tension was the FBI's refusal to assume the responsibility vested in the agency by federal law to investigate major crimes on the reservation. The FBI chose instead to act, in Special Agent Norman Zigrossi's words, as a "colonial police force," to repress the challenge to Wilson's power.

Based solely on documented political deaths, the yearly murder rate on the Pine Ridge Reservation during the three years after the confrontation at Wounded Knee (March 1, 1973, to March 1, 1976) was 170 per 100,000. By comparison, Detroit, the reputed "murder capital of the United States" at the time, had a murder rate of 20.2 per 100,000 in 1974. The United States average was 9.7 per 100,000, with the range for other large cities as follows: Chicago, 15.9; New York City, 16.3; Washington, D.C., 13.4; Los Angeles, 12.9; Seattle, 5.6; and Boston, 5.6. An estimated 20,000 persons were murdered in the United States during 1974. In a nation of 200 million persons, a murder rate comparable with that of Pine Ridge between 1973 and 1976 would have left 340,000 persons dead for political reasons in one year, 1.32 million in three years.

The struggle that resulted in so many violent deaths was also taking place within the realm of tribal politics. When Wilson sought reelection in 1974, Russell Means, an Oglala who had helped found AIM, challenged him. In the primary, Wilson trailed Means, 667 votes to 511. Wilson won the final election over Means by fewer than 200 votes in balloting that the U.S. Commission on Civil Rights later found to be permeated with fraud.

In December 1976, after a long legal battle, AIM leader Leonard Peltier was sent back to the United States to face charges of murdering two FBI agents at Pine Ridge, South Dakota. In this photo, Peltier is led to a helicopter that will take him from Canada to the United States.

For two years following the 1973 confrontation at Wounded Knee, traditional Indians had suffered great losses. Much of the violence had occurred when armed men in cars suddenly appeared and started shooting. By June 1975, there had been more than sixty unsolved murders of traditional Indians and AIM supporters at Pine Ridge, and many community members were frustrated by the lack of response from the FBI. In this climate of fear and helplessness, with the U.S. government offering no protection, the traditional Indians appealed to AIM for protection. AIM was determined to fight back.

On June 26, 1975, two FBI agents, new to the area and unknown to its residents, dressed in plain clothes and each driving an unmarked car, reported that they were following a red pickup truck that they believed contained a man who was wanted for stealing a pair of boots. The vehicle actually contained a load of explosives destined for an encampment of about a dozen members of the American Indian Movement not far from Oglala.

When the two FBI agents followed the red pickup off the road and into a field, a point within earshot of the encampment, a firefight erupted between the agents and the vehicle's occupants, who have never been identified. Armed only with their handguns, the agents attempted to get their rifles out of the trunks of their cars and in doing so exposed themselves to the gunfire.

Hearing the shooting and thinking themselves under attack, men and women from the encampment came running, carrying rifles. They took up positions on a ridge overlooking the vehicles. They were fired at and they fired back. Bullets filled the air.

Within a few minutes, a third FBI agent arrived. This agent had been some fifteen miles (twenty-four kilometers) away and had driven to the scene at more than 100 miles (160 kilometers) an hour. But the first two FBI agents lay dead near their vehicles. The red pickup fled the scene, but not before it had been seen and reported and the report preserved in the records of FBI radio transmissions.

The AIM members up on the ridge went down to the vehicles, where they discovered the bodies of the two FBI agents. Bewildered and frightened, they fled the area on foot under heavy fire, as law enforcement authorities began arriving in large numbers. An Indian man lay dead. He had been shot through the head at long range. The two FBI agents, already wounded, had been shot through the head at point-blank range.

In the months that followed, the FBI launched an all-out campaign to exert its control over Pine

Following Leonard Peltier's sentencing to two life terms in prison, many of his supporters have attempted to convince the government to investigate improprieties in the case brought against him.

Ridge and to find the red pickup. It was unable to find the red pickup or its occupants, however. Three men who had been at the AIM encampment that day, Darrelle Butler, Bob Robideau, and Leonard Peltier, were arrested and charged with killing the two FBI agents. No one was ever charged with killing the Indian. Peltier fled to Canada, where he fought extradition (being handed over) to the United States by the Canadian authorities. In the meantime, Butler and Robideau were tried and acquitted by a jury who believed they had acted in self-defense and that they had not been the ones who executed the wounded agents. The fury of the government then fell on the third defendant, Leonard Peltier.

Documents obtained by perjury and coercion were presented to the Canadian authorities to obtain Peltier's extradition. At Peltier's trial, the red pickup now became a red and white van, resembling one that Peltier could be linked to. FBI agents who had filed reports the day of the shooting reporting the red pickup now contradicted their own testimony, saying their reports had been in error. The government now claimed that the two dead FBI agents—who had reported that they were following a red pickup—did not know the difference between a red pickup and a red and white van.

With the first trial as a blueprint for everything it had done wrong in court, the government found a sympathetic judge in another jurisdiction. The new judge made rulings favorable to the prosecution that the first judge had denied and also made rulings against the defense that the first judge had allowed. The new judge also did not allow testimony about the climate of violence and fear on the reservation, thus effectively thwarting the defense's case of self-defense. By withholding crucial FBI ballistics evidence from the defense and from the court showing that Peltier's weapon had not fired the fatal shots, the government got a conviction against Peltier. He was sentenced to two life terms in the federal penitentiary at Fort Leavenworth, Kansas.

— B. E. Johansen / D. L. Birchfield

SEE ALSO:
American Indian Movement; Black Hawk; Butler, Darrelle; Cortés, Hernán; *Incident at Oglala;* Indian Major Crimes Act; Keokuk; Means, Russell; Peltier, Leonard; Red Cloud; Robideau, Robert; Sitting Bull; Wilson, Richard; Wounded Knee, Confrontation at (1973).

SUGGESTED READINGS:
F.B.I. *Uniform Crime Reports*. Washington, D.C.: Government Printing Office, 1975.
Matthiessen, Peter. *In the Spirit of Crazy Horse*. New York: Viking, 1983.
Johansen, Bruce E. and Roberto F. Maestas. *Wasi'chu: the Continuing Indian Wars*. New York: Monthly Review Press, 1979.
Weir, David, and Lowell Bergman, "The Killing of Anna Mae Aquash," *Rolling Stone*, April 7, 1977.

PLANTS

SEE Indian Medicines; Native American Contributions.

PLENARY POWER

This term is used to describe the control that the Congress of the United States claims to have over Indian affairs. In the United States Constitution, in article 1, section 8, clause 3, known as the Commerce Clause, Congress is granted the power to regulate commerce with foreign nations, among the several states, and with the Indian tribes. In article 2, section 2, clause 2, known as the Treaty Clause, the president and the Senate are given the power to make treaties, including treaties with Indian tribes.

According to the United States Supreme Court, these two clauses provide Congress with complete control over Indian affairs. In addition, the Supreme Court gives two other reasons for its contention that the federal government has the right to govern Indians: (1) the discovery doctrine (discovery of North America by Europeans and conquest of its inhabitants) in international law; and (2) the doctrine of trust responsibility in Indian treaties, which contains a guarantee that the federal government will protect the treaty tribe and, therefore, must regulate the Indians for their own protection.

In 1824, Congress created the first federal agency to administer Indian policy, the Office of Indian Affairs, within the War Department. In 1849, Congress transferred the office to the Department of the Interior. In 1947, the office was renamed the Bureau of Indian Affairs (BIA). The executive officials, including the president and the secretary of the interior, cannot establish Indian policy but only administer the Indian policy established by Congress.

The Supreme Court claims that the power of the Congress over an Indian tribe is virtually unlimited. In *United States v. Sandoval* (1913), the Supreme Court states: "[T]he questions whether, to what extent, and for what time they [Indian tribes] shall be recognized and dealt with as dependent tribes requiring the guardianship and protection of the United States are to be determined by Congress, and not by the courts."

According to the Supreme Court, Congress has the power under the Commerce Clause to terminate a tribe. Between 1954 and 1966, Congress passed legislation that authorized the secretary of the interior to terminate its trust responsibility with Indian tribes and its members. The secretary of the interior terminated many tribes by either distributing all of the tribe's property to its tribal members or to the tribal corporation, if one had been established. The Congress claims that its power over tribal assets is nearly absolute. After termination, the federal government ended its supervision over a tribe, the tribal government was abolished, and tribal members were subject to state law. The termination policy was slowly relaxed in the 1960s and early 1970s. A bill introduced in Congress in 1977 called for the termination of every Indian tribe, but that bill did not pass.

Because the Bureau of Indian Affairs can determine the eligibility requirements of tribal members for an Indian program, it therefore controls tribal membership—and the size and strength of a tribe—when it creates a program. In land compensation claims, Congress can distribute the award according to the tribal membership established by the tribe or by its own standard.

A portrait of Pocahontas. Since her own day, the name, face, and life of this Powhatan woman have been an almost-legendary source of fascination and intrigue to non-Native artists, writers, and, more recently, moviemakers.

The Congress also claims that it has the power to regulate all private property of Indians, but that it chooses not to do so. Trade and liquor are regulated by laws passed by Congress, including federal licensing requirements for all persons, except full-blood Indians who trade on an Indian reservation. Also, federal employees involved in Indian affairs may not trade with Indians. Congress gave federal officials the jurisdiction over certain serious crimes (murder, manslaughter, rape, assault with intent to kill, arson, burglary, and larceny) within Indian country. Most recently, the Indian Gaming Regulatory Act of 1988 was passed to regulate gambling on Indian reservations.

SEE ALSO:
Bureau of Indian Affairs; Indian Gaming Regulatory Act of 1988; Indian Major Crimes Act; Indian Trade and Intercourse Acts; Termination Policy; Tobacco.

POCAHONTAS (1595–1617)

The life of Pocahontas, daughter of a powerful Powhatan chief, is one of the most deeply rooted stories of the United States' past. Much of what is known about Pocahontas's early life is taken from the writings of Captain John Smith, an explorer with the Virginia Company.

It was the Virginia Company that, in 1607, established the first permanent English settlement, called Jamestown, located on the shores of the James River in Virginia near Chesapeake Bay. One of the most famous legends depicted during this time was that of the circumstances surrounding the capture of John Smith. According to Smith's accounts, he was taken prisoner by the Powhatans and narrowly escaped death through the intervention of Pocahontas who, in effect, saved his life.

Smith's accounts of this event have been widely questioned by modern historians, and it is possible that Smith misinterpreted the events. One theory suggests that Smith was being initiated into tribal membership, wherein a mock execution like

This painting of Pocahontas, based on a 1616 engraving by Simon van de Passe, depicts Pocahontas, following her journey to England, in a style befitting British royalty.

the one Smith describes takes place. During the execution, a sponsor must speak out for the one being initiated. Pocahontas would have served as Smith's sponsor, and it is argued that this interpretation better explains her behavior toward the English colonists.

Pocahontas served as a liaison between her people and the English, but, despite her aid in negotiations, relations between the parties eventually deteriorated. The major breakdown of relations between the English and Powhatans occurred in January of 1609, when the Powhatans grew suspicious of the English as a result of the growing numbers of settlers. It was believed that the English intended to take even more land away, and the Powhatans forbade any further trading with the colonists. This placed the English in jeopardy because they depended upon the Powhatans for their food.

According to several accounts, Pocahontas was a betrayer of her people because she took the role of protector of the English, warning them of the Powhatans' plans to destroy them. It is unknown what Pocahontas's motives were—whether she felt a responsibility toward the English she had sponsored or whether she had a personal love for Smith.

After Smith departed for England, negotiations broke down further between the colonists and Powhatans. In 1612, Pocahontas was taken captive, held in Jamestown, and used as a bargaining tool for the freedom of the English imprisoned by Chief Powhatan. During her stay at Jamestown, Pocahontas was converted to Christianity and baptized. She was also courted by the colonist John Rolfe, whom she later married in 1613. The marriage brought a period of peace between the Powhatans and settlers.

In 1616, Pocahontas sailed to England with Rolfe to be presented to the king and royal court. She was received as a princess and daughter of an emperor. While in England, Pocahontas's health began to fail. In March of 1617, on a return trip to her homeland, Pocahontas died in the port of Gravesend, at the mouth of the Thames River, in England. She left behind her husband and her son Thomas.

SEE ALSO:
Jamestown; Virginia.

POKAGON, SIMON (1830–1899)

Simon Pokagon, a son of Chief Leopold Pokagon of the Pokagon band of Potawatomis, has long been credited as the author of *O-gî-mäw-kwe Mit-i-gwä-kî, Queen of the Woods*, which was first published in 1899, the year of his death. In recent years, his authorship of this novel—which was first written in the Algonquian language—has been called into question. Set in the Great Lakes region, the novel is the autobiographical story of Pokagon and his courting of and marriage to Lonidaw. In the novel, the couple's two children are both destroyed by alcohol and by contact with the European-American world. Pokagan has also been credited with writing nonfiction books about Algonquian legends.

Scholar James A. Clifton, who has studied the Pokagon band of the Potawatomi people, writes that Pokagon "was scarcely literate and had grave difficulty composing a simple letter" ("Simon Pokagon's Sandbar: Potawatomi Claims to Chicago's Lakefront," *Michigan History* 71, no. 5 [1987]: 14). Clifton also writes that *Queen of the Woods* was probably written by the wife of Cyrus Engel, Pokagon's attorney, agent, publisher, and advisor. Several contemporary scholars, including Louis Owens (*Other Destinies: Understanding the American Indian Novel*, University of Oklahoma Press, 1992), have cited Clifton's findings in their own work.

PONCA

Historically, the Poncas lived in earth-covered lodges in permanent villages in a number of places, including Minnesota and the Dakotas, particularly in the Black Hills of South Dakota. Mainly farmers, they occasionally went on seasonal buffalo-hunting expeditions. They also warred with their traditional enemies, the Sioux (Dakota, Lakota, and Nakota) Nations.

In 1858, the Poncas ceded their land claims to the United States and were assigned a reservation near the mouth of the Niobrara River. Boundaries between the Ponca and Sioux Nations were set. But in 1868, Ponca lands were ceded to the Sioux by the Fort Laramie Treaty of 1868 that established the Great Sioux Reservation. The result was dev-

Métis in the Second Riel Rebellion. The Métis were descendants of French traders who had married Native American women before Canada was established as a confederation. Riel proposed establishing a provisional government in Saskatchewan; the Canadian authorities forcefully objected. Throughout much of the 1870s and 1880s, the alliance proposed by Riel to establish this government engaged in the most widespread unrest of Canadian history on the frontiers of the nineteenth century.

Poundmaker had initially urged peace, but his young warriors pushed him into raids on settlements and a brief (but successful) battle with three hundred soldiers. The uprising was short-lived, however, because the newly constructed railroad allowed the Canadian government to transport a large number of troops into the area in a short time. Riel's second rebellion was crushed in a few days; Poundmaker was arrested and sent to prison. After serving one year of a three-year sentence, Poundmaker became ill and was released. He died four months later.

SEE ALSO:
Canada, Native–Non-Native Relations in; Métis; Riel, Louis.

POWHATAN

SEE Jamestown; Pocahontas; Roanoke Island Natives and Roanoke Colony; Virginia.

POWWOWS

Powwows are Native American events that take place all over the United States and Canada. A powwow can be held just about anywhere—in a school gymnasium, on a reservation, or in a city auditorium. For Indian people, powwows are a time to celebrate, give thanks, honor elders, and meet with friends through singing, drumming, and dancing.

Powwows are a celebration of Indian culture, held throughout the year to mark various events. For example, the Annual Pawnee Homecoming Powwow in Oklahoma over July 4 honors veterans. The annual Crow Fair and Rodeo in Montana is advertised as "Tipi Capital of the World." Poplar, Montana, holds an annual Oil Celebration Powwow. The Lac Courte Oreilles Chippewa (Ojibwe) of Wisconsin hold an annual Honor the Earth Powwow in July. The North American Indian Days, hosted by the Blackfeet tribe in Brown-

A group of young dancers in regalia, one featuring the U.S. flag, perform at a powwow on the Warm Springs Reservation near Mt. Hood, Oregon.

ing, Montana, are an annual powwow event. And Native student unions in universities usually sponsor an annual powwow.

Exactly when the modern powwow began is uncertain. Throughout Native American history, however, celebration through song and dance goes as far back in time as one can imagine. Today's powwow can be traced for a hundred years through definite developmental periods and is continually expanding in scope and popularity. The word *powwow* has its origins from an Algonquian word, *pau-wau*, which means a conjurer or medicine man. When Europeans observed healing ceremonies of the pau-wau (pronounced PAW-waw), accompanied by dances, they mispronounced the name as powwow and assumed that it referred to any gathering of Indian people. The word *powwow*, like many other Indian words now a part of the English language, was adopted by Indians and non-Indians alike.

A young girl proudly displays her jingle dance dress with handmade bells at a Connecticut powwow.

Historically, North American Indian tribes held ceremonies and dances to celebrate successful hunts, food gathering, and warfare. Other ceremonies included name-givings, adoptions, coming-of-age rites, and honor ceremonies for deceased relatives. Many times, celebrations were held to reestablish allegiances and friendships with visiting tribes. The celebrations were often accompanied by dancing and feasting. Summer reunions were especially important to many Indian tribes, taking place at prearranged locales and dates. Tribal members came together for social activities and religious ceremonies that helped to reaffirm their unity. Cultural traditions became strengthened with these gatherings. The powwows of today evolved out of these religious and social dances.

Some of the earliest recorded powwows began with the Ponca Fair and Pow Wow held in 1877 in Oklahoma. This dance lasted four days and brought people from far and wide. The Anadarko Fair began somewhere around 1916, and, in 1925, the Haskell Institute in Lawrence, Kansas, first began a world's championship dance contest. The Annual Red Bottom Celebration at Fraser, Montana, began in 1903.

During the time of the so-called Indian Wars in the late 1800s, the United States government was disparaging of Indian practices and encouraged repression of Native culture and traditions. Native

A group of Apache dancers perform at a public powwow in New Mexico. With its many indigenous cultures, New Mexico has a full calendar of powwows and other Native gatherings throughout the year.

people were sent to live on reservations, their freedom became increasingly restricted, and their Native identities were diminished. Native languages and ceremonial practices like the Sun Dance were forbidden by law. Indian children were taken away from their families and sent to learn the European-Americans' way in boarding schools. Traditional Native lands were seized and made available for white settlements. Food rations were limited or didn't make it to the reservations at all, and blankets infected with smallpox were distributed to Indian people. These ill-disposed measures were attempts to ensure that Indian people and their many cultures would die out. A U.S. Department of Interior circular to all reservation superintendents in regard to Native dancing emphasized that ". . . the Native dance still has enough evil tendencies to furnish a retarding influence and a troublesome situation . . . the dance is apt to be harmful and we should control it by educational processes as far as possible, but if necessary by punitive measures."

By the late 1930s, mission schools and the influence of the federal government had nearly eliminated Native languages, lifestyles, religions, and customs. However, the government wasn't successful in wiping out either social or religious dances.

Negative attitudes toward Native Americans began to waver in the late 1940s and early 1950s as World War II ended. Many Indians were veterans, and Native clans and societies honored the veterans through powwows—a practice that still continues today. With the 1960s civil-rights movement, Native pride underwent bold new changes. Native communities experienced a rejuvenation in regard to traditional practices, and powwows are the greatest example of this renewed vitality.

Today, powwows range from the very large to the very small and happen just about all the time throughout the United States and Canada. However, it is during the summer months that powwows are most frequent. People who devote their time to traveling all over the country often refer to the powwow season as "the powwow trail." Traveling the powwow circuit and competing in dance contests for big cash prizes, selling crafts and food, or playing in drumming and singing groups are for some people a way to earn their living or supplement their incomes. Powwows are attended by Indians and non-Indians, the young and the old, reservation Indians and urban Indians, out-of-towners and locals, dancers and spectators—just about anyone who wants to experience Indian culture is welcome.

An Aztec dancer from Mexico performs at a New England powwow that has attracted participants from throughout the Americas.

A hoop dancer performs at a powwow held at Taos Pueblo, New Mexico.

The northern Plains–style powwow begins with opening ceremonies. This is the time when the dancers enter the arena dressed in their dazzling outfits and finery for the grand entry. The dancers are staged according to their dance category and follow the military veterans, who carry a variety of flags, including the U.S. flag. During the grand entry, the attendants and spectators all stand for the host drum flag song, which is an Indian version of a national anthem. Following the veterans into the dance arena are an assortment of dignitaries such as tribal officials, powwow princesses, state politicians, and honored guests. Following the dignitaries are the different categories of dancers and contestants—the male traditionals and female traditionals, the men's fancy dancers and the female fancy shawl dancers, the grass dancers, jingle dress dancers, and others. After the flag song is over, usually a spiritual elder offers a prayer, and the powwow dancing events are underway.

At the center of every powwow lies the drum. A drum group comprises five or more people, and, depending on the size of the powwow, the number of drum groups performing will vary. Each powwow has a host drum. The host drum is placed closest to the announcer's stand. Along with drumming, the drum groups also sing many different kinds of songs—traditional or new—such as trick songs, songs that stop and start suddenly, and shake songs. In southern powwows, the snake, buffalo, and stomp songs are common. The northern style powwow songs for the intertribal dance, grass dance, fancy dance, and traditional dance songs vary in tempo from slow to very fast. Each song is sung in repetitions of four, and the words can be in English or an Indian language or replaced with vocables (syllables that carry the melody). The names of some drum and singing groups are the Teton Travelers, Kicking Woman Singers, The Eagle Whistles Drum Group, and Rocky Boy Singers.

Tribes in the Southwest have their own dancing and singing styles. The Navajos, for instance, have a couples dance called the squaw dance. Other Arizona tribes, such as the Tohono O'odhams (Papagos) and the Pimas, dance to music called chicken scratch, which reveals Mexican influences. The nations of Oklahoma, such as the Cherokees and Creeks, have the stomp dance. In Alaska, Native Alaskans dance the Red River jig to fiddle music, which has its origins with the Hudson's Bay Company traders.

The contest dancing is held in a variety of different ways, depending upon the number of competitors in each category. In cases where there are many competitors, the judges go through a process of elimination until the final dance-offs, which are held on the last day of the powwow. The average prize for winning a dance category such as the men's traditional is somewhere between three hundred to five hundred dollars, although sometimes the cash prizes can be as much as one thousand dollars. One of the most compelling of the dance categories is the men's fancy dance, which developed out of Plains Indian war dances of long ago. A fancy dancer must have stamina and quick, well-choreographed footwork to be a good dancer. The fancy dance costume is also one of the most elaborate and includes brightly colored double-feather bustles.

A young Shoshone woman at a Shoshone/Bannock powwow in Idaho.

Each dance category is identified by the style of costume and dance steps. The grass dancers, for example, are immediately recognized for their colored yarn fringe layered on matching shirt, pants, and aprons, and the dance movements consist of side-to-side swaying motions. The jingle dancers wear rows of tin cones lined on their dresses, and the dance is quite active, with a great deal of twisting and turning in order to get the full effect of the jingles.

Powwows continue to flourish among communities all over the United States and Canada. These celebrations provide immediate access to and understanding of Native cultures and maintain Native identity and continuity in times of great change. The powwow schedules for most tribes and reservations, including their availability to the general public, may be obtained from tribal offices.

— T. Midge

SEE ALSO:

Boarding Schools; Dance, American Indian; Music and Musical Instruments; Pan-Indian (Intertribal) Movements; Singing.

SUGGESTED READINGS:

Braine, Susan. *Drumbeat Heartbeat: A Celebration of the Powwow*. Minneapolis: Lerner Publications Company, 1995.

Davis, Mary. *Native America in the Twentieth Century: An Encyclopedia*. New York: Garland Publishing, Inc., 1994.

Heth, Charlotte. *Native American Dance: Ceremonies and Social Traditions*. Washington, D.C.: Fulcrum/Smithsonian, 1992.

Roberts, Chris. *Powwow Country*. Helena, MT: American & World Geographic Publishing, 1992.

A young buffalo dancer practices at a Project Head Start class at Laguna Pueblo, New Mexico.

would therefore become citizens of the United States at the conclusion of the Mexican-American War in 1848, the only Indians in the Southwest to gain U.S. citizenship in that manner. Most Indians in the Southwest did not become U.S. citizens until the Indian Citizenship Act of 1924. Pueblo peoples today are still to be found in their ancestral homeland, primarily along the upper Rio Grande Valley in the state of New Mexico, along with the Hopis in northeastern Arizona, and in the small community of Isleta del Sur near El Paso, Texas, just across the border from New Mexico.

Pueblo people are at home in both their Native world and in the world of the dominant American culture. They have learned to be U.S. citizens while still remaining Pueblo. Changes, however, have been inevitable. Pueblo culture has long been multilingual and is now rapidly becoming bilingual. In times past, Pueblos might be fluent not only in the language of their pueblo, but also in one or more of the other Pueblo languages or dialects. With the arrival of the Spanish, Pueblos also learned the Spanish language. With the arrival of the Comanches in their vicinity, many Pueblos, especially those on the eastern frontier nearest the Plains, learned Comanche, just as some northern Pueblos learned Jicarillan due to close relations with the Jicarilla Apaches. Pueblos nearest the Navajos were apt to know Navajo. Spanish is still common among older Pueblo people. But increasingly, Pueblo young people are only learning the language of their pueblo and English. With English being a universal language within the region, and with its hold growing ever stronger by the profound linguistic influences of radio, television, print journalism, and public education, few Pueblos learn other Native languages today besides their own.

In religion, Pueblos have modified Christian teachings to make them compatible with traditional views. The result is a form of Christianity found nowhere else in the world, a Pueblo Catholicism. It has much in common with the experiences of

The designs on this drummer's beaded regalia reflect his Mexican origins. The event is a harvest dance at San Ildefonso Pueblo, New Mexico.

Native peoples throughout the middle and southern portions of the hemisphere who are nominally Catholics, but whose practice and beliefs are at great odds with official laws and beliefs. The Church is tolerant of this practice, having found after great effort that it cannot uproot traditional Pueblo religious beliefs. The Church made its greatest effort to do so with public hangings and whippings in the 1660s and 1670s. In the Pueblo Revolt of 1680, twenty-one of the thirty-three Catholic priests in New Mexico were killed. One of the reasons that Pueblo religion is so entrenched is that there is no word for "religion" in the Pueblo languages. To be Pueblo is to live a way of life, to hold a world view, to be a part of a community.

Ceremonial dances are at the heart of Pueblo culture. Pueblo traditional dance costumes are among the most striking of any Native peoples. Kachinas are masked male dancers who represent spirits of nature and who perform ceremonial rituals in the plazas on feast days and other important occasions. Ritual clowns are also a part of some ceremonials. The clowns engage in outlandish behavior—funny, sexual, and absurd. Some ceremonials, such as the Zuni Shalako, feature kachinas in ten-foot- (three-meter-) high costumes. Among the Hopis, the kachinas are said to live in the San Francisco peaks near Flagstaff. They come to the Hopis for six months each year, arriving during the February Bean Dance.

Pueblo culture is matrilocal and matrilineal; a married couple lives with or near the wife's mother, and children are born into the mother's clan. Wife abuse is uncommon in functioning matrilocal cultures because the wife is surrounded by the protection of her relatives. Child custody disputes are unknown because the child is a member of the mother's clan and remains with the mother or her relatives should a marriage not endure. Related women, and their husbands and children, live in clusters of apartments within a larger structure, which is a classic description of both Anasazi and Pueblo building requirements. The development of this matrilocal system of residence accounts for the change from pit houses to aboveground masonry apartments. A remnant of the pit house survives as the kiva, an underground chamber that is built into the apartments of the Southwest. In the kivas, related men meet and hold ceremonies. Such

Contemporary dwellings based on traditional architecture at Taos Pueblo, New Mexico.

meeting places afford an important opportunity for maintaining ties among fellow clan members in matrilocal societies, because even though men in a particular clan are related (tracing their descent through the female line), they live apart from one another in the homes of their wives.

The Pueblo people are among the most successful dry farmers in the world, and they are also skilled at irrigation farming. Today, many Pueblos continue the agricultural traditions of their ancestors and continue to cultivate in the same time-honored manner.

Many Pueblo people are also employed in the urban areas near their homes, and many of them who now live in these urban areas return to the pueblo frequently, sometimes as often as nearly every weekend. Traditional craftwork in pottery, weaving, jewelry, and drum making are also important sources of income.

Tribal enterprise also provides jobs. The Hopi Cultural Center, with its restaurant and motel, offers some employment opportunities. At Acoma, the visitor center has a restaurant, a crafts shop, and a museum; a bingo hall is nearby. Cochiti provides services for the town of Cochiti Lake, which leases its land from Cochiti Pueblo and has a commercial center, a marina, and an eighteen-hole golf course. The majority of Isleta's residents work in Albuquerque, but others operate the bingo hall, grocery stores, and the campgrounds at Isleta Lakes. Some excellent vineyards are found at Jemez. Laguna Industries, Inc., manufactures communications shelters for the U.S. Army and is only one of a number of Laguna tribal industries. Some Lagunas found employment in the uranium-mining industry, and others are now finding employment in the reclamation project that is attempting to restore the mined land. Many of Nambé's residents work in Santa Fe, in Espaniola, or at Los Alamos National Laboratory. Others are employed by the Eight Northern Indian Pueblos Council. Picurís Pueblo Enterprise Cultural Center operates guided tours and houses a museum, a restaurant, and a store. Pojoaque generates revenue by the development of a commercial strip fronting the highway; the pueblo also operates an official state tourist center.

The Sandia Indian Bingo Parlor is one of the largest in New Mexico. Sandia also operates Bien Mur Indian Market Center and Sandia Lakes Recreation Area. At San Ildefonso is a museum, several trading posts, and a visitor center, as well as the annual Eight Northern Indian Pueblos Artist and Craftsman Show. At San Juan is the Oke Oweenge Crafts Cooperative. At Santa Ana, there is the Ta Ma Myia crafts shop. Santo Domingo is developing commercial property along Interstate 25, where it also operates a museum. Taos operates a horseback-riding and guided-tour business as well as several trading posts. Tesuque operates a bingo parlor and Camel Rock Campground. Zuni has been a model for tribal enterprise, taking advantage of direct federal grants through the Community Action Programs to gain administrative control of almost all of the Bureau of Indian Affairs (BIA) contract services on the reservation, which now run more efficiently and with much greater community commitment and participation.

Under the Indian Reorganization Act of 1934, many Pueblos refused to allow their traditional form of government to be replaced by a foreign system (a tribal council system modeled somewhat after the U.S. government, but also having much in common with the way corporations are governed). Each tribe within the United States was given the option of reorganizing under the act, and many Pueblos refused to do so. Traditional Pueblo government features leadership from different sources of strength within each community. Clans are an important force in providing leadership, and, among some Pueblos, specific clans have traditional obligations to provide leaders. This is true of the Bear Clan among the Hopis, the Antelope Clan at Acoma, and the Bow Clan at Zuni. The Tewa pueblos have dual village leaders, where the heads of the winter and summer social groups each exercise responsibility for half the year.

In matters of traditional religion, which includes many activities that European-Americans associate with government, a cacique, or leader, among the Pueblos and a kikmongwi among the Hopis

A collection of Cochiti Pueblo storytellers by artists Rita Lewis, Helen Cordero, and Ada Suina *(left to right)*.

A delegation of Pueblo Indians from New Mexico poses near the U.S. capitol with their U.S. government hosts in this 1923 photo. They were in Washington, D.C., to meet with the Senate committee on public lands to protest U.S. policies regarding the Pueblo people.

have serious responsibilities to the people. Along with their assistants, they not only perform ceremonies but also organize hunts and the planting of crops. Today, the Hopis in Arizona and six New Mexico pueblos (Isleta, Laguna, Pojoaque, San Ildefonso, Santa Clara, and Zuni) elect their governors and councils. In New Mexico, the All-Indian Pueblo Council had its first recorded meeting in 1598, when Juan de Oñate met with thirty-eight Pueblo leaders at Santo Domingo. Pueblo oral history recounts that the various pueblos had been working together long before the arrival of the Spanish and that secret meetings of the council were a major factor in the successful planning of the Pueblo Revolt of 1680. The All-Indian Pueblo Council had its contemporary public origins on November 5, 1922, when Pueblo leaders assembled at Santo Domingo to meet with U.S. government officials. Its present constitution was adopted on October 16, 1965. The council is a confederation of New Mexico pueblos that seeks to protect and advance their interests, particularly regarding relations with other governments.

Pueblos had to sue to have their status as Indians recognized by the United States, which was achieved by a decision of the United States Supreme Court in 1916. They are now federally recognized Indian tribes. By joining together to form the All-Indian Pueblo Council in the 1920s, after a congressional investigation had revealed that twelve thousand non-Pueblo claimants were living on Pueblo land, they succeeded in getting the U.S. Congress to pass the Pueblo Lands Act of 1924, which secures some of their traditional land to them.

The struggle for water rights has characterized much of their relations with the government of the United States in this century. In 1975, after a struggle of thirty years, Taos Pueblo succeeded in regaining its sacred Blue Lake and fifty-five thousand acres (twenty-two thousand hectares) of surrounding land in the mountains above the pueblo. This marked one of the few times that the United States has returned a major sacred site to Indian control.

— D. L. Birchfield

John Marcus, a Taos Pueblo elder.

SEE ALSO:
Acoma Pueblo; All Indian Pueblo Council; Anasazi; Arizona; Coronado Expedition; Encomienda; Hopi; Indian New Deal (Indian Reorganization Act of 1934); Isleta Pueblo; Kachina; Mexican-American War; New Mexico; New Spain; Oñate Expedition; Pueblo Revolt of 1680; Southwest Literature, Contemporary; Taos Pueblo; Tewa Pueblo; Tiwa Pueblo; Towa Pueblo; Zuni.

SUGGESTED READINGS:

Forbes, Jack D. *Apache, Navaho, and Spaniard.* Norman: University of Oklahoma Press, 1969 and 1994.

Ortiz, Alfonso, ed. *New Perspectives on the Pueblos.* Albuquerque: University of New Mexico Press, 1985.

Ortiz, Alfonso. *The Pueblo.* New York: Chelsea House, 1994.

Sando, Joe. *Pueblo Nations: Eight Centuries of Pueblo Indian History.* Santa Fe, NM: Clear Light Publishers, 1992.

Trimble, Stephen. *The People: Indians of the American Southwest.* Santa Fe, NM: Sar Press, 1993.

PUEBLO REVOLT OF 1680

Nineteen villages make up the Rio Grande Pueblos in northern and central New Mexico. They first experienced European contact in 1536, when the Spaniard Alvar Núñez Cabeza de Vaca and his group of settlers made their way across Texas to New Spain after a failed attempt to settle Florida. Upon hearing De Vaca's tales of great riches to the north, Viceroy Antonio de Mendoza appointed Franciscan friar Marcos de Niza and his Moroccan slave Estevanico to lead a new expedition. The Marcos-Estevanico expedition reached the Pueblos in 1539. Fray Marcos viewed the Pueblos from a distant hill and hurried back to New Spain.

In 1540, Francisco Vásquez de Coronado led a large expedition in search of the fabled Seven Cities of Cibola. Coronado found neither gold nor the seven cities and returned to New Spain with a disappointing report. Between 1581 and 1595, several small expeditions explored the region, until finally, in 1598, a contract for the colonization of the Pueblos was awarded to Juan de Oñate. Oñate settled on the Rio Grande at the Yunque-Yungeh Pueblo, renaming it San Gabriel. He visited all of the pueblos, inviting each cacique, the spiritual head of the pueblo, to swear allegiance to the king of Spain and to accept Christianity.

Oñate began the process of Christianizing the Pueblos. By 1631, there were approximately sixty-six missionaries working among the Pueblos, with the goal of converting all of the Pueblo peoples to Christianity. Traditional religious practices among the Pueblos were banned, and Native religious leaders were often executed for conducting rituals and dances that the Spaniards considered idolatrous. The Spanish civil authorities also exacted taxes and labor from the Pueblos. This system of forced labor was called the *encomienda* system.

Don Pedro de Peralta, Oñate's successor as governor, moved the capital to Sante Fe in 1610 and continued a rigorous program of converting the Pueblos to Christianity. Over the next few decades, the Spanish civil authorities and the missionaries were increasingly at odds with each other concerning the exploitation of the Pueblos. The governors, who were gradually bringing the Pueblos into a state of slavery, complained that the missionaries were mistreating and punishing the people unnecessarily. The missionaries, on the other hand, wrote to the authorities in Mexico City that the governors were using the Pueblos as a cheap labor source for personal gain, undermining their own "benevolent" goals of Christianization.

In 1660, a severe drought occurred in the region. Overgrazing of the Spaniards' cattle and the subsequent erosion of fragile irrigation systems compounded the drought's severity. And with the drought came attacks from the Plains tribes. Before Spanish colonization, the Pueblos enjoyed relative peace with the neighboring Apaches, Navajos, and Comanches. With the drought affecting tribes across the Southwest, creating hunger—and the Spanish with their cattle, sheep, and pigs as a possible food source—the Pueblos became a vulnerable target for increasing numbers of raiding parties. The Spaniards had promised to defend the Pueblos, but there was little they could do. By 1670, the colony was close to the starvation level.

It seemed that the Christian God had brought little more than starvation and ruin to the Pueblos, and, in the early 1670s, the Pueblos returned to their traditional religious customs and rituals,

The Salinas archaeological site in New Mexico. Abandoned by its inhabitants in the late 1600s, this site is an example of the unique blend of Pueblo Indian and early Spanish-American influences in the region around the time of the Pueblo Revolt of 1680.

including the public Katcina (Kachina) dances. The missionaries considered this to be witchcraft and paganism, and, in 1675, Governor Francisco de Treviño arrested forty-seven medicine men and spiritual leaders of the Pueblos and brought them to Sante Fe to stand trial. Four of the men were executed for practicing sorcery, and the others were whipped and jailed.

This event, coming on the heels of drought, raids, and famine, led the leaders of the scattered Pueblos to unite for the first time and begin plans for a general rebellion. Among those who had been jailed was a medicine man named Popé, of the San Juan Pueblo. Over the next five years, Popé enlisted the aid and cooperation of almost every village for an organized revolt.

The revolt was planned for August 11, 1680, but on August 9, two messengers bearing details of the uprising were captured, and the plan was put into execution a day early. This brief warning did allow some of the missionaries and settlers to flee. At dawn on August 10, 1680, the Pueblo people rose against their Spanish colonizers, killing many and forcing many to flee. Most of the Franciscan missionaries were killed immediately, including those in the Taos, Picurís, San Cristobal, Santo Domingo, Hopi, and Zuni pueblos.

Governor Antonio de Otermín learned of the revolt and fled with hundreds of colonists to Sante Fe. For five days, thousands of Pueblo warriors laid siege to the fortified city. Eventually, Governor Otermín and the surviving settlers were able to escape and make their way south to El Paso del Norte, on the north bank of the Rio Grande. Through the course of the rebellion, the Pueblos killed twenty-one missionaries and approximately four hundred Spanish colonists.

For twelve years, the Pueblos were again in control of their land, though they were more vulnerable to raids by neighboring Apaches and Navajos. In 1692, General Diego de Vargas visited the Pueblos and returned with the conviction that the region could be recolonized. In 1693, de Vargas and over a thousand soldiers stormed Sante Fe and reclaimed

After returning home, Pushmataha drummed up his own expedition, which proved disastrous. He was caught by surprise in an ambush by a much larger force in the far western lands, and all of his companions were killed. He alone escaped. Rather than return home immediately, he spent a considerable amount of time in the region, some accounts say as much as three to five years, learning the seasonal movements of his enemies, who have never been satisfactorily identified. All this time, he seethed with a desire for revenge. When Pushmataha finally returned home, he drummed up one expedition after another, most of them successful, devoting years to the undertakings, until his reputation within the nation as a military leader was unexcelled.

The most influential event of his life probably occurred in 1790, when a delegation of Choctaw leaders was invited to travel to Philadelphia, which was then the U.S. capital. It is not certain that Pushmataha was a member of this particular delegation, but it is known that he did travel to the U.S. capital fairly early in his career. During the trip, the young Choctaw leader was awestruck by the immense resources, industrial capacity, and population of the young nation. Realizing that it would be suicidal for his country to ever engage in hostilities against such a powerful foe, the hallmark of his statesmanship for the rest of his life became a policy of peace with Euro-Americans, at any cost.

Responding to pressure from United States treaty commissioners in 1805 for the Choctaws to remove themselves to land west of the Mississippi River, Pushmataha entered into another feverish period of military exploits in the West. This period lasted for several years and may have had a role in the complete depopulation of the southeastern portion of the present state of Oklahoma, which is the area where the Choctaws were eventually removed to in the early 1830s. The grim spectacle of Choctaws making a place for themselves in the West is an area of United States removal policy that has not been adequately studied. Pushmataha also waged war against his bitter personal enemies, the Osages, during this time.

On the eve of the War of 1812, he met the Shawnee leader Tecumseh in debate in Choctaw Country and convinced his people to expel Tecumseh from their country and to remain loyal to the United States. In the War of 1812, he led hundreds of Choctaw troops as a lieutenant colonel in General Andrew Jackson's U.S. Army, fighting engagements against Tecumseh's allies, the Red Stick faction of the Creeks, and against the British at the Battle of New Orleans.

At the negotiations for the Treaty of 1820, Pushmataha displayed his exceptional knowledge of the geography of the Far West. He corrected General Andrew Jackson's U.S Army maps, which mistakenly showed that the headwaters of the Red River (which are east of the front range of the Rocky Mountains) lay as far west as the headwaters of the Canadian River (which are found in the high mountains of northeastern New Mexico).

As leader of the Choctaw delegation, Pushmataha helped negotiate the agreement that became the Treaty of Washington of 1825. He died of the croup on December 24, 1824, in Washington, D.C., and was buried in the Congressional Cemetery with full military honors by the United States.

— D. L. Birchfield

SEE ALSO:
Choctaw; Jackson, Andrew; Removal Act, Indian; Tecumseh.

PUYALLUP

The Puyallup Reservation is located in Pierce County of Washington State, with its tribal headquarters in Tacoma, Washington. The tribe has 1,800 enrolled members, with 927 living on-reservation. The reservation contains 18,062 acres (7,315 hectares). It was established by the Medicine Creek Treaty in 1854 and enlarged by executive order in 1857 and 1873.

The tribe adopted a constitution in 1936 and established a tribal council of five elected members, each serving a three-year term. The Puyallup tribe was at the forefront of the struggle to retain fishing rights, and it is a member of the Northwest Indian Fisheries Commission.

Puyallup tribal legends say that the tribe came into being many thousands of years ago in the foothills of the Cascade Mountains behind what is now Sumner, Washington. As the glaciers in the region receded, the Puyallups moved to the shores of Puget Sound, living there peacefully for hundreds of years. The tribe's name in its own Salish language is Spwiya' laphubsh, which means "generous and welcoming behavior to all peoples, friends, and strangers who enter the land of the Puyallups."

It was this generous behavior that caused so much difficulty for the Puyallup people. The reservation, which was reserved for the Puyallups, was coveted and taken away by land-grabbers. At first, the Puyallups saw opposing this theft as not being generous to the strangers who seemed to need land. Over time, the Puyallups ceded large portions of their territory to the government. Parts of the cities of Tacoma, Milton, and Puyallup, and all of the city of Fife, are located on the Puyallup Reservation.

Most recently, the tribe has opened up many claims in court in an attempt to regain lost land. The tribe has currently agreed to set aside many of those claims for a negotiated agreement with the state of Washington, the city and port of Tacoma, and other parties. This settlement should allow the tribe to improve the economic condition of its people.

SEE ALSO:
Fishing Rights; Washington Coast and Puget Sound Indians, History of.

QUAKERS

The Religious Society of Friends, widely known as Quakers, was founded in England in approximately 1652 by George Fox. The Quakers were just one of several religious groups that arose in seventeenth-century England in protest against the domination of the church by the state. They also opposed certain church doctrines and ceremonies that were similar to practices in the Roman Catholic faith.

The Quakers wore plain clothing, modeled after the clothes of working people. They used plain speech as a means of protesting against what they viewed as the meaningless formalities and lavishness of speech at that time. Quakers, led by Fox, believed that God existed in every person and that by following this Inner Light, a person could discover true belief without the help of a minister.

A Friends' (Quaker) meetinghouse in colonial Pennsylvania.

QUILLWORK AND QUILLWORKERS

As early as the sixth century B.C.E., Native peoples of North America decorated their clothing and belongings with bird feathers and the long needle-like spines of a slow-moving and largely nocturnal rodent, the porcupine. Of these two sources of quills—birds and porcupine—porcupine quills were more frequently used. The porcupine is found in a vast geographic area, extending throughout wooded regions from Pennsylvania to Washington State and from Alaska to New Mexico.

Quillwork flourished as a craft during the nineteenth century and is largely associated with Plains tribes, especially the Siouan Nations. A number of other tribal groups have quillworking traditions, including the Arapahos, Assiniboines, Blackfeet, Cheyennes, Crees, Ojibwes (Chippewas), Omahas, Pawnees, and Poncas.

These people traded quills at intertribal gatherings, and, as a result, quills were also used by southern tribes such as the Hopis and Zunis. Tribal groups attribute the development of quillwork to various mythological or legendary figures. The Blackfeet believe that the Thunder Spirit brought them the knowledge of how to embroider with quills. Deer Woman, a Lakota woman, was instructed through a dream, and Buffalo Woman brought quillwork to the Cheyennes.

Before quillwork could be created, quills had to be plucked, washed, sorted, dyed, and dried. Boys or men hunted the porcupine, usually killing it. Shortly afterward, while the porcupine's body was still warm, women pulled the quills from its body. The porcupine was subsequently dressed, cooked, and eaten. An adult porcupine may have from thirty thousand to forty thousand quills on its tail, back, neck, and belly. Quills are essentially hollow tubes, one to five inches (over two to thirteen centimeters) in length. They are white in color for one-half to two-thirds of their length, turning gray to dark brown toward the sharp tapering end of the spine. The largest and thickest quills are found on the porcupine's tail; the shortest and thinnest are from the belly.

This Sioux pouch, crafted around 1875, features porcupine quillwork with a central thunderbird image surrounded by a pattern of feathers.

Quillwork forms the basis of this beaded barrette.

Women prepared the quills, first cleaning them by soaking them in soapy water. They often dyed the quills bright colors by boiling them in water containing flowers, moss, roots, berries, nuts, wood ash, bark, and, sometimes, human urine. Wild sunflowers were used to make a yellow dye. Wild grapes or walnuts produced a black dye, and buffalo berries created red. Later, quillworkers dyed quills using commercial dyes or scraps of dyed cloth.

Women sorted quills and stored them according to their length in separate baskets or bags made of the bladders of large animals. Immediately before using a quill, the woman flattened it by pulling it between her thumbnail and her forefinger or through her clenched upper and lower teeth. She might hold one or more quills in her mouth to soften them with saliva so they would bend more easily.

Typically, a quillworker gathered the following supplies in preparation for her work: sorted bags of quills; a knife to trim the sharp quill barbs; thread; paint and a stick or a scraper to impress designs; a bone, thorn, horn, or metal awl to punch holes; a piece of bone or antler to flatten the sewn quillwork; and the prepared bark or animal skin. Quillworkers followed patterns painted, scraped, or poked on the surface to be decorated. Since quills are short and stiff, most quillwork designs are geometric, following square, rectangular, and triangular shapes.

Among the Arapahos and Blackfeet were quillworker societies that restricted quillworking within the tribe to those members who were instructed first by older women. The societies helped ensure consistency in quillwork methods, designs, and motifs. Tribal groups developed distinctive quillwork, preferring particular techniques or patterns. The northern Arapahos, for example, preferred round shapes, stars, and forms resembling the large letter X. Some quillwork embroidery designs were in the shapes of flowers and resembled the patterns in calico cloth.

These Pomo dancers in California wear headbands made with porcupine quills.

Quillworkers used four methods of decorating with quills. Quills were wrapped, sewn, woven, or braided. In wrapping, quills were twisted around round-shaped objects, such as the stems of pipes or around human or animal hair. Quills were braided—much as hair is braided—around sinew threads by alternately folding a quill in half to the left and then to the right. Sewn quills were embroidered on tanned animal skins by twisting or folding quills over thread made from grasses or sinew from the tendons of large animals such as elk, buffalo, and moose. After sewing, the quillworker would press down on the quills to further smooth and flatten them. In weaving, quills were interlaced, over and under, like weaving a mat. Quillworkers faced difficulty in concealing the ends of quills and producing a uniform and even surface. Quillwork, especially work using dyed quills, gives a bright and shiny appearance.

Quillworkers often incorporated other materials alongside quills, such as moose hair, buffalo wool, trading beads, or grasses. Quillwork was used to decorate clothing, such as shirts, dresses, or moccasins, and quillwork designs were often prepared in strips that could then be sewn as borders around arm holes or around neck holes. Quills were also applied to ornaments, such as round rosettes, that could be attached to objects such as infant cradleboards. Wrapped quillwork was used to decorate objects such as pipe stems, quivers, and knife sheaths. Quills used in jewelry such as earrings and necklaces were often not flattened, thus retaining their tubular or cylindrical shape.

By the late nineteenth century, quillwork was largely replaced by beadwork using glass trading beads. However, quillwork, like beadwork and other Native crafts, is currently experiencing a revival in interest.

—L. Roy

SEE ALSO:

Baskets; Beadwork and Beadworkers; Cradleboards; Feathers and Featherwork; Jewelry, Native American; Moccasins; Regalia.

SUGGESTED READINGS:

Bebbington, Julia M. *Quillwork of the Plains; Le "Travail aux Piquants" des Indiens des Plaines*. Calgary, Alberta: Glenbow-Alberta Institute, 1982.

Lyford, Carrie A. *Ojibwa Crafts*. 1943. Reprint, Stevens Point, WI: R. Schneider, 1982.

———. *Quill and Beadwork of the Western Sioux*. 1940. Reprint, Stevens Point, WI: R. Schneider, 1984.

MacDonald, Fiona. *Plains Indians*. New York: Barrons Educational Series, 1992.

Parker, Arthur C. *The Indian How Book*. 1927. Reprint, New York: Dover, 1975.

Patterson, Lotsee, and Mary Ellen Snodgrass. *Indian Terms of the Americas*. Englewood, CO: Libraries Unlimited, 1994.

Taylor, Colin F., ed. *The Native Americans: The Indigenous People of North America*. New York: Smithmark, 1991.

QUINAULT

The Quinault Indian Nation is located in Jefferson and Grays Harbor Counties in Washington State. The Quinault Reservation sites include 208,150 acres (84, 301 hectares), and the Quinault Nation is made up of seven tribes: the Quinault, Queets, Hoh, Ozette, Chehalis, Chinook, and Cowlitz tribes. The nation has an enrolled membership of 2,280, with 943 members living on-reservation. The nation's headquarters is in Taholah, Washington.

The tribes that make up the Quinault Indian Nation have lived along the Quinault River and in portions of the Olympic Peninsula for thousands of years. This region was very rich in natural resources, especially fish, and particularly salmon. With this natural bounty, the Quinaults had time to develop a society rich in tradition and supported by a stable and consistent form of governance.

At the later part of the 1700s, first contact with Europeans began to alter elements of Quinault society, and the tribes began to deal with new social, religious, economic, and political structures. On July 1, 1855, a party of Quinaults, headed by the leader Howyat'l, signed the Quinault River Treaty with representatives of the United States. The treaty was signed by Washington Governor Isaac Stevens and was ratified by the U.S. Senate and signed by President James Buchanan. Under the treaty, the Quinaults ceded claims to vast regions of land in exchange for maintaining some territory and in exchange for fishing, gathering, and hunting rights; certain provided goods and services; and perpetual protection provided by the United States. Under this treaty, the meaning of "Quinault" was redefined. For thousands of years, Quinault had referred to the people who lived along the Quinault River. But when, under the Quinault River Treaty, other tribes moved onto the Quinault Reservation, they became part of the Quinault Nation and took on that name.

Today, in order to be a Quinault, one must verify at least one-quarter combined heritage from one of the seven designated tribes (Quinault, Queets, Quileute, Hoh, Chehalis, Cowlitz, or Chinook) and not be a member of any other Indian tribe or nation. Individuals who cannot meet this blood quantum requirement are allowed to apply for tribal adoption.

In 1873, the Quinault Reservation was enlarged by executive order. In 1934, the Quinault Nation accepted the Indian Reorganization Act of 1934, and in 1975, the nation adopted a new constitution.

The Quinault Nation has battled to preserve rights granted to it by treaty, especially fishing rights. The Quinault Nation, in order to maintain its rights, participates in the Northwest Indian Fisheries Commission.

SEE ALSO:

Indian New Deal (Indian Reorganization Act); Washington Coast and Puget Sound Indians, History of.

REAGAN SPEECH IN MOSCOW, 1988

On May 30, 1988, shortly before the end of his second term as president of the United States, Ronald Reagan was answering questions for students at Moscow University when he said that perhaps the "American people" should not have "humored" Native Americans by allowing them, as Reagan put it, "to live a primitive lifestyle." Reagan was

President Ronald Reagan's comments in the Soviet Union about assimilation and American Indians set off a wave of objections from Native groups and advocates.

reacting to the students' assertions that the United States was playing up dissidence and protest in the Soviet Union while suppressing it among American Indians and other peoples of color in the United States.

Reagan's comments ignited a storm of protest among Native American leaders. Susan Harjo, executive director of the National Congress of American Indians, said that Reagan had invoked outdated stereotypes about American Indians. John Red Horse, director of the American Indian Studies Center at the University of California–Los Angeles, said that Reagan's remarks showed his own ignorance of American history and treaty law.

Joe de la Cruz, president of the Quinault Indian Nation (on the coast of Washington State), said, "The president . . . does not understand the reason for treaties, which are part of the law of the land. American history does not teach the part that the Indians played in the formation of the United States Constitution." With these words, De la Cruz echoed a position that has been a source of interest and some controversy among historians: that many of the eastern confederacies, most prominently the Iroquois, helped shape concepts of freedom, federalism, and pluralism on which the United States was founded.

On June 8, Reagan refused to retract the comments.

At the time, many critics of Reagan's speech said that it showed how little the Reagan administration cared about improving conditions for American Indians. During the 1980s, several of the poorest areas of the United States were on Indian reservations; counties in South Dakota that comprised the Pine Ridge and Rosebud Reservations were the poorest in the country. Such criticism continued throughout the presidency of George Bush but relented under President Bill Clinton, who held a summit meeting of more than three hundred tribal representatives at the White House on April 29, 1994.

SEE ALSO:
Iroquois Confederacy; Social Conditions, Contemporary; White House Meeting, 1994.

REBURIAL AND REPATRIATION OF HUMAN REMAINS AND SACRED OBJECTS

Since time immemorial, ancient burial grounds of Indian people have become exposed by erosion of the land and river floodings. In more recent times, individuals and companies come across human remains and burial objects while developing the land that they have acquired. Until recently, these remains were often sold to museums and individual collectors—usually for a high price—and the items were placed on display for the world to view. Because of the handsome price museums and individuals were willing to pay for ancient Indian items, grave robbing became almost commonplace well into the twentieth century and, by the 1980s, reached a level that many Native people considered epidemic.

This Native burial site at Taos Pueblo, New Mexico, carries signs of both Native and early Spanish spiritual influences.

In 1990, in large part as a response to the outcry coming from the Native community over the desecration of their burial grounds, the United States government passed the Native American Graves Protection and Repatriation Act. (*Repatriate* means "to return to one's country.") Even before the passage of the act, however, many state historical societies, museums, companies, and private collectors had begun returning recovered skeletal remains to Indian tribes for reburial. In one instance, a museum in the Northeast notified the Lakota people that it had in its possession the remains of Indian people who had been killed in the 1890 massacre at Wounded Knee, South Dakota. The Lakotas sent an elder to the museum, and she notified officials that the remains had to be taken back to the Wounded Knee cemetery so that the people buried there could be at peace. In the hands of their descendants, the human remains are given a proper, traditional burial. According to many traditional beliefs, when a burial site is desecrated and the items are removed from the site, the spirit of the person cannot be at peace. With the proper burial, the spirit may be at peace again.

In addition to ancestral human remains, many organizations and individuals have also been returning objects that are sacred to their tribes. In many cases, Native people were—and are to this day—buried with these sacred objects. Many of these objects have been taken from burial grounds by people looking for artifacts and archaeological evidence. In the 1800s, however, when United States soldiers killed Indian men, women, and children, they often took with them human remains or personal items as battle "trophies." These items, which included

A group of Arapaho Indians carries out its mission of repatriating human remains that had been removed from a traditional burial site.

headdresses, articles of clothing, fans, rattles, shoes, weapons, and other personal possessions, often found their way to museums or historical societies all across the country. Many of these institutions have come to understand the sacred and culturally significant nature of these items and, at the request of tribal officials, have returned them to the tribes to which their owners once belonged.

Under the care and guardianship of tribal authorities, some tribal governments have created their own museums where people may view the items and gain a better understanding of their purpose. Today, with the passage of the Native American Graves Protection and Repatriation Act, increasing numbers of sacred objects have found their way back to their people.

SEE ALSO:
Native American Graves Protection and Repatriation Act; Wounded Knee (1890).

RED CLOUD (1822–1909)

Red Cloud (Mahpiua-Luta) was a leader and prominent war chief among his people, the Oglala Sioux. An ambitious mediator between his people and the U.S. government, Red Cloud was among the Indian leaders responsible for the signing of the Treaty of Fort Laramie in 1868.

Red Cloud was born in 1822, and it is said that on the day of his birth, a red meteorite flashed across the sky—an event that inspired his name. Red Cloud's father was Lone Man and his mother was Walks As She Thinks. Soon after Red Cloud was born, his father died, and Red Cloud was raised by his mother's uncle, Smoke. Red Cloud gained a high rank among his people at an early age in recognition of his bravery and clever war tactics against such Sioux enemies as the Pawnees and Crows. When Red Cloud was nineteen years old, he shot his uncle's rival, Bull Bear, who was a powerful

Oglala chief. It was exploits like these that soon propelled him toward his leadership position among his people.

A historic photograph, taken in the 1880s, of Red Cloud *(front row, far right)* with other Indian leaders of the northern Great Plains, including *(front row, left to right)* Sitting Bull, Swift Bear, and Spotted Tail. These men were instrumental in struggles against U.S. government forces in the Northern Plains.

The time period between 1866 and 1868 became a time of turmoil for Red Cloud and the Sioux, when what is known to some as Red Cloud's War took place between Indians and the United States. During the 1860s, Euro-American settlers and U.S. military personnel attempted to construct forts along what became known as the Bozeman Trail. Since the trail's "discovery" by John Bozeman in 1863, settlers and miners had made their route through the passage illegally, as much of the trail crossed through lands that were reserved by treaty for the Sioux and Cheyennes. The illegal passage of whites through Indian lands resulted in many confrontations and battles led by Red Cloud and his allies over control of the region. Finally, in 1868, the Fort Laramie Treaty was signed, and the U.S. government agreed to relinquish the Bozeman Trail in exchange for peace between the Indians and whites. This treaty was soon disregarded, however, when, in 1874, a mining expedition led by George Armstrong Custer invaded the land of the Black Hills following the discovery of gold.

In 1870, Red Cloud and other Indian leaders visited Washington, D.C., to meet with President Ulysses S. Grant and then went on to New York City, where Red Cloud gave a public speech. As a result of his diplomatic efforts, the government established the Red Cloud Agency (now known as the Pine Ridge Reservation) in present-day South Dakota. Other Sioux leaders, notably Sitting Bull and Crazy Horse, considered Red Cloud a "sell-out" to the white man and the U.S. government because of his willingness to comply with what they considered only the government's "proposed" land reserves and food rations. Red Cloud maintained steadfastly that he was intent upon ensuring peace and survival for his people, however, and that he was through with war. In 1872, he sent this message to Sitting Bull and the other chiefs: ". . . I shall not go to war anymore with the whites. I shall do as my Great Father [President Grant] says and make my people listen . . . you must carry on the war yourselves. I am done."

Although Red Cloud resisted war, he continued fighting for Indian rights. In his later years, he

Every year, the parade opening Oklahoma City's Red Earth Festival attracts thousands of visitors, many of them non-Indian tourists.

lost his sight and was baptized in the Catholic Church. He died in 1909.

SEE ALSO:
Black Hills; Bozeman Trail and the Battle of a Hundred Slain; Cheyenne; Crazy Horse; Crow; Custer, George Armstrong; Fort Laramie Treaty of 1868; Pawnee; Siouan Nations; Sitting Bull.

RED EARTH FESTIVAL

The Red Earth Festival, which began in 1987, is the biggest Indian-based tourist event in the state of Oklahoma and has been dubbed by its sponsors, the Oklahoma Department of Tourism, as one of the largest and grandest Indian festivals in the world. The three-day event, held every June in downtown Oklahoma City, draws thousands of people from around the world to enjoy activities such as Indian fashion shows, an art show and sale, dance troupes, storytellers, choirs, free artist demonstrations, and film and video showings.

The festival is also host to Native powwow dancers, singers, and artists who compete for a total of eighty-five thousand dollars in prize money. Arts and crafts booths fill the auditorium at Oklahoma City's huge Myriad Convention Center, and the participants' work is presented through a variety of gallery shows, film festivals, and museum exhibitions. Winners of the art contests have their work on display throughout the festival.

Top names in Native music and dance are also drawn to the Red Earth Festival, providing spectators with a huge array of Native entertainment. The events begin with a parade of nations through downtown Oklahoma City, where the tourists may see tribal representatives and dancers in full regalia. Although the festival clearly caters more to tourists than to American Indians, the Native dancers, artists, and vendors benefit from the gala event as well. Also, in addition to the art and entertainment, the festival also features a symposium on the issue of tribal sovereignty.

SEE ALSO:
Tribal Sovereignty.

RED JACKET
(c. 1760–1830)

This portrait of Red Jacket depicts the Seneca leader in European attire.

Red Jacket, a nephew of Handsome Lake, was a major Iroquois leader during the late eighteenth and early nineteenth centuries. He was best known as an ally of the British in the American Revolution. A Seneca, Red Jacket's first name was Otetiani, meaning "He Is Prepared." Later, he took the name Sagoyewatha, meaning "He Causes Them to Be Awake." The name *Red Jacket* came from a scarlet coat given to him by the British for fighting with them during the American Revolutionary War.

Red Jacket's skills lay more in diplomacy than in waging war. After he fled the battle of Oriskany in 1777, avoided battle at Wyoming Valley in 1778, and made an early exit at the Battle of Newtown in 1779, Red Jacket developed a reputation as a coward. At another point during the American Revolution, Red Jacket killed a cow and smeared his tomahawk with blood to convince other Iroquois that he had killed a Euro-American man. Instead, Joseph Brant and Cornplanter ridiculed Red Jacket as a "cow killer."

After the war, Red Jacket reconciled his differences with the Americans, unlike Joseph Brant, who moved to Canada. In 1792, Red Jacket was among a number of Iroquois chiefs invited to Philadelphia to parlay with George Washington. In the War of 1812, he fought on the U.S. side against the British.

Regardless of his allegiances, Red Jacket believed that Indians should retain their own lands and cultures. He sought, and sometimes got, extensive legal protection for reservation lands. His speeches in defense of Native rights have been cited by generations of Iroquois.

In 1821, Red Jacket sent a letter to De Witt Clinton, governor of New York, enumerating the problems that the Iroquois were having with settlers, including illegal cutting of timber on Indian lands, poaching of livestock, the death of fishing stocks because of dam building, and the decrease in hunting animals. "The greatest source of all our grievances is, that the white men are among us," Red Jacket concluded.

In his last years, Red Jacket became alcoholic and was deposed as an Iroquois chief in 1827. The chieftainship was restored shortly before he died on January 20, 1830, in Seneca Village, New York.

SEE ALSO:
American Revolution; Brant, Joseph; Cornplanter; Handsome Lake; Iroquois Confederacy; Seneca.

RED POWER

SEE American Indian Movement; American Indian Resistance; *Incident at Oglala;* Trail of Broken Treaties; Wounded Knee, Confrontation at (1973).

RED SHOE (? – c. 1750)

Red Shoe, also known as Shulush Humma and Shulushamastabbe, was a war chief of the Okla Falaya tribal division of the Choctaw Confederation. He was the most influential Choctaw leader during the disastrous Choctaw Civil War of 1747 to 1750, which ranks with the removal of the Choctaws in the 1830s as one of the two most traumatic events in Choctaw history.

The Choctaw Civil War had its beginnings in the annihilation of the Natchez Indians by the French in the 1730s, the flight of the remaining Natchez to the protection of the Chickasaws, and the subsequent military action of the French and their Choctaw allies against the Chickasaws. In seeking to end hostilities with the Choctaws, the Chickasaws offered to help make better trade goods available to the Choctaws. The Chickasaws traded with English merchants of the Carolinas, who had higher quality and less expensive trade goods. James Adair, the resident English trader among the Chickasaws, who would later publish a book in England in 1775 about his life with the Indians, tried hard to win the Choctaw trade from the French.

Red Shoe pursued an alternating policy of peace or war with the Chickasaws, depending upon the situation at any given time, but he listened to Adair's overtures during times of peace. When a French trader among the Choctaws raped Red Shoe's wife, Red Shoe killed the trader and became more receptive to the idea of trading for British goods. When the French put a price on his head, he shifted his allegiance entirely and entered into discussions with Adair and other English representatives from the Carolinas.

The French resisted the loss of their trade monopoly with the Choctaws and sent troops into the Choctaw Country to prevent English traders from entering. Factions among the Choctaws developed, and civil war broke out in 1747.

The war divided the Choctaw Confederacy in half. The Okla Falaya and about half of the villages of the Okla Hannali sided with the English. The Okla Tannap and the remaining Okla Hannali villages sided with the French. The small Okla Chito tribal division, in the center of the nation, which historically had provided the Choctaws with its most able leaders, appears to have been caught between the warring factions and annihilated. They cease to appear in historical records as a separate tribal division after the war.

The war was prosecuted by the Choctaws with more deadly thoroughness than most Indian wars. Fortunes shifted depending upon which faction had most recently been supplied with powder and lead. Once, when the English faction had almost won against the French, the English faction were not resupplied by the English colonials in the Carolinas. A complete turnabout ensued. Red Shoe was assassinated by a rival Choctaw, and the Choctaws realized that they were exterminating themselves for the benefit of the Europeans and ceased hostilities—but not before the French faction had achieved a decisive advantage in the fighting.

As a result of the war, the Choctaws were so weakened that they participated very little in the French and Indian War of 1755 to 1763, when the French were expelled from the continent by the British. Another result of the war was that the Choctaws resolved never again to allow themselves to be divided by Europeans. They henceforth gained a reputation for skill at playing one European power against another, lessons in diplomacy that had been learned at a high cost.

SEE ALSO:
Choctaw; French and Indian War; Removal Act, Indian.

These Comanche dancers display regalia combining modern and traditional materials and designs at San Ildefonso Pueblo, New Mexico.

REGALIA

Historically, members of most Native American cultures have viewed their clothing not only as a way of keeping comfortable, but as an important means of self-expression. Regalia—clothing or decoration that is worn to demonstrate rank and bearing, or that is intended to display a sense of style or finery—often indicates the wearer's social status by its design and ornamentation. Highly imaginative regalia may completely alter one's appearance, and when used as a part of a ceremony, it may have a striking effect on both the wearer and other participants and observers—so striking that the wearer may appear to have become a supernatural being. In certain tribes, clothes decorated in a specific manner traditionally indicated the person's honored position within the tribe, be it military society official, medicine person, member of a special social group, or one who has performed with distinction in battle. How one dresses is still taken seriously in Native cultures, and participants in dances, powwows, and traditional ceremonies take considerable pains to put to the best use many striking and varied costumes. Dress and the decorations used to make it attractive may still be used to command respect, attention, and admiration, and even to frighten people into submission, although many of these uses are more for ceremonial than everyday purposes.

Before what would become the permanent presence of Europeans in the Americas in the late 1400s, the natural environment provided all the materials needed to make and decorate Native clothes. Color depended on the availability of natural materials for dyes, and texture resulted from the different kinds of tanned hides or fibrous grasses used to weave clothing. Other natural decorative materials were used to make interesting sounds as the wearer walked about the camp. The most popular materials for creating these sounds, before the introduction of tiny hawk bells, were deer hoof or dewclaw rattles.

Contact among the tribes was common, and trade goods were passed from coast to coast as desirable items found their way across the continent. Cowrie shells were popular among Lakota-Dakota women to decorate their dance dresses, in spite of the fact that their homeland, the Black Hills area, was landlocked. These women had no access to the sea, where the shells originated, but cowries made their way inland in the bags of traders, first Indian and then European.

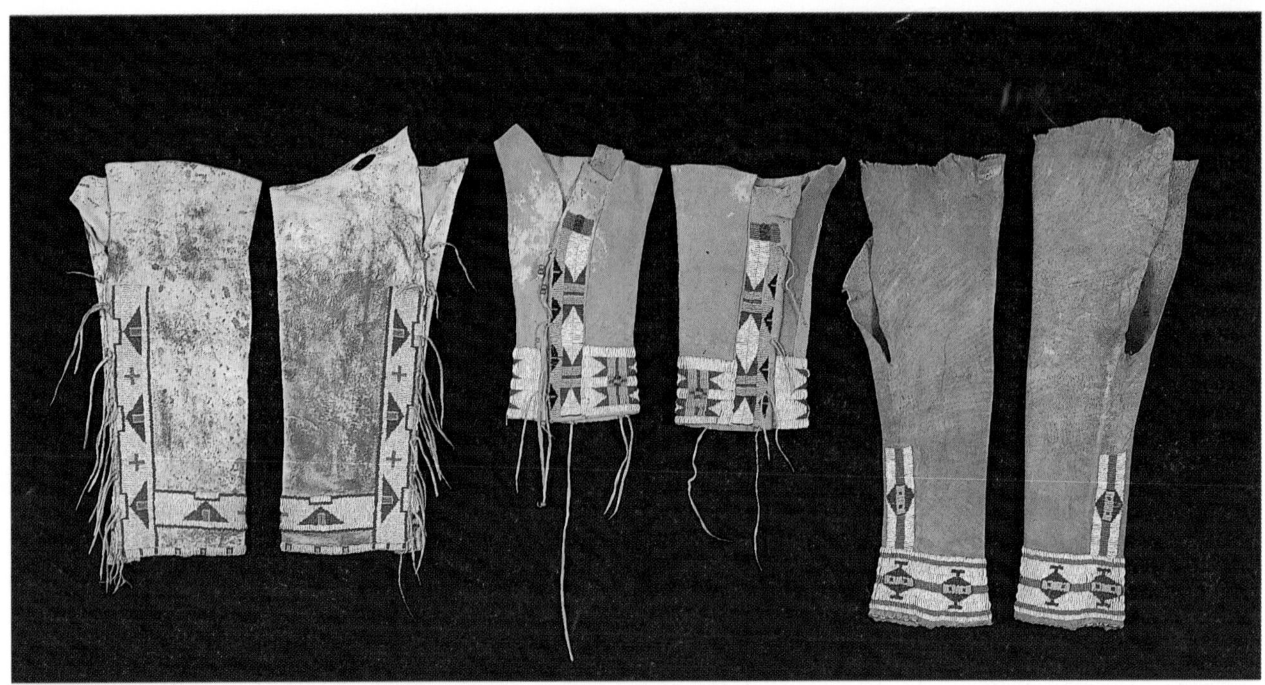

Several varieties of women's leggings, all of them crafted around 1880 and featuring beadwork and painted designs on tanned deerskin. The pair on the far left is Cheyenne in origin, and the other two pairs are Arapaho.

One article of clothing that seemed to be common to all tribes is the breechclout (also known as a breechcloth or a loincloth). Perhaps early contact among various Native peoples was responsible for the universal appeal of the breechclout, or the idea was such a commonsense approach to dressing that it evolved in all tribes, more or less on its own. A breechclout is always made from a single long piece of skin or cloth, and it can be decorated in the manner of any particular tribe. The eastern woodland tribes have traditionally used ribbon work and beaded floral patterns on the breechclout, while the Plains Tribes have used ribbons, beaded geometric patterns, and sometimes even painted designs in bold colors on theirs.

Leggings, the tubular coverings for legs, are another pan-Indian and unisex article of clothing. They once were used to protect the legs from the elements, as well as from insect bites and bush scratches. Decorated to match a dress, women's leggings are only knee high. Men's leggings are much longer, coming high up on the thighs. Some are combined with moccasins to make one piece. Like the breechclout, leggings are made from stroud wool or skins and are usually decorated with ribbons, silver, or beads.

Thread is an important and necessary ingredient for dressmaking in any culture. Before traders came to the Americas, Native women used sinew (animal tendons) and fibers from nettles, hemp, and tree bark that could be twisted into threads. Before the advent of steel needles, women used sharp instruments called awls, which were made of sharp deer or buffalo bones. Some also used long thorns from trees like the locust or thorn apple. Instead of pushing the needles through the material, they punched holes with them and pulled the thread through the materials by hand.

With increased contact between Indians and Europeans, dyes from Europe slowly replaced the natural ones found in the Americas. Roots, buds, flowers, seeds, and berries, as well as juices from boiling bark and nutshells, were used for thousands of years to give color to ornaments and clothing alike. Materials to be colored were boiled, then rinsed and boiled again until the desired color could be seen. Red was obtained from bloodroot, wild plum, and red ochre, which is a red clay. Bloodroot also made yellow and orange; lamb's quarters (a type of weed also known as pigweed) yielded shades of green; rotted maple leaves gave purple; and black and brown came from oak and hazel burrs, walnut husks, or earth.

Feather bustles stand out as part of the regalia of this Shoshone/Bannock powwow dancer.

Beaded regalia worn by a Navajo woman at a Shoshone/Bannock powwow in Idaho.

Moose hair and porcupine quills were used for decoration of clothing before the introduction of trade beads in the middle of the seventeenth century. Moose hair embroidery was practiced mainly by the woodland Indians. The hair was about four to five inches (ten to thirteen centimeters) long and taken from the mane, cheeks, and rump of the moose. It was then washed, dyed, moistened, and flattened to be sewn on the object to be decorated. In contrast, porcupine quills were used by both eastern and western tribes. Some were used in their natural cylindrical shape, and others were flattened by pulling them through the front teeth—carefully. They were then dyed and sewn onto moccasins, bags, knife sheaths, and dresses. Some Indian women are able to perform this method of decoration today, but it is uncommon and very expensive.

Glass trade beads eventually replaced these older methods of decoration. The beads came in several sizes: large beads for necklaces, pony (small) beads for sewing, and, later, the popular tiny seed beads that are used on clothing. Many bead designs were taken from old moose hair embroidery and quillwork. Later, beadwork was combined with shiny silk ribbons to make the garment or item even more attractive.

The earliest wool cloth came from France and England. The most plentiful of the woolens traded in America was primarily made in Stroudwater, Gloucester, England. Although wool cloth first appeared in the eastern areas of North America, it became popular throughout the entire continent and was used for blankets, breechclouts, and dresses in many tribes. This coarse strouding, as it was named, was manufactured just for American Indians. The two colors, bright red and dark navy blue, came from dyeing the cloth rather than weaving from colored yarns. The old cloth that manufacturers used for this material was of poor quality, and often the dye ran when it was exposed to the rain. Today, Indians still use imported stroud cloth from England. The wool is of very high quality and is quite expensive. It comes in many colors, although the traditional red and navy blue are still among the most popular for clothes and blankets.

By the eighteenth century, calico, linen, and muslin were popular trade goods among the Indians of the Great Plains and eastern part of the continent. These fabrics, along with woolens like stroud cloth, began to replace the animal skins that Indians once wore. Some Native women began to dress in the manner of the white settlers, with long cloth skirts and full sleeved blouses. The so-called Five Civilized Tribes (Cherokee, Chickasaw, Choctaw, Creek, and Seminole), which were from the southeastern part of the United States, adopted the settlers' style of dressing, but with important differences. For example, the Creeks—and also the Shawnees—added silver hair combs with floor-length ribbons, and the Seminoles created unique piecework fabrics for both men and women, as well as silver or beaded decorations for clothing or moccasins. It is important to note that although they used the same fabrics and similar styles as Euro-Americans, Native Americans adapted the garments to be a unique symbol of their tribal identity, using the same kind of decorations that were used on their skin clothes. Sometimes the men kept the skin leggings and breechclout but adapted western dress for the rest of their outfits. It is not unusual to see an Indian man, when dressed in traditional regalia, with a cloth ribbon shirt, animal skin or stroud cloth leggings, and breechclout.

This dramatic Cayuse horse mask was fashioned in 1870 out of red wool trade cloth and decorated with polished buffalo horns, yellow dyed horsehair, and beaded stars. It is representative of the kind of parade regalia used on horses by Native peoples of the Northern Plains and Plateau regions.

Another important feature of Native dress is the Pendleton blanket. First made in Pendleton, Oregon, at the turn of the nineteenth century, the blanket, with its pan-Indian designs, appealed to Native people throughout North America. Pendleton blankets became a significant trade item and a symbol of a family's wealth. Today, it is an indication of high esteem to receive a Pendleton blanket in a powwow giveaway or at a ceremonial. Pendleton even sells baby blankets for the youngest children. Natives and non-Natives alike use these traditional blankets not only on beds but on their backs as well. They are made into striking coats and vests for everyday use by those who enjoy functional beauty.

A slab bearing rock art seems to usher visitors into a cave at Petroglyph State Park, New Mexico.

While Stone Age rock art has been found and studied in areas throughout North, Central, and South America, archaeologists consider three areas to be most important. The first and oldest is the Patagonia area of Argentina, the next is the area in and around Arizona once inhabited by the Anasazi, and the third is the wide expanse of the rest of North America a few centuries before Europeans arrived. The Indian groups dominating these areas were all advanced hunting cultures, some nomadic and some that settled and also took up farming.

Patagonian Rock Art

Archaeologists estimate that the rock paintings found in the caves and gorges of Patagonia date back to around 9000 to 8000 B.C.E. Most of these paintings are silhouettes of hands, usually stenciled in shades of red with black, although yellow and brown paint were also used. In some areas, the inhabitants of ancient Patagonia also painted human and animal figures in hunting and dancing scenes believed to represent the magic of tribal priests. The third kind of rock art they produced was a geometric design that incorporated shapes like dots, rays, circles, crosses, arrows, and wavy lines. Some included human footprints and the tracks of animals. These designs, also painted mostly in red and black, were apparently used for decoration as well as for ritual magic. Some people believe the hand stencils were found in such large numbers throughout the area because they were symbols of initiation rites of young men into tribal society. Others believe the hand paintings could have been the ritual imprints of people about to be sacrificed to the gods.

The Rock Art of the Anasazi

The Anasazi, or "ancient ones," lived in the Southwest, in what is today the Four Corners region—the desert area where the states of Utah, Arizona, New Mexico, and Colorado all adjoin. This area is

Pictographs at Temple Wash, Utah, appear to represent a ceremony performed by local residents.

vations. In 1883, Crow Dog became the defendant in a murder case that is still cited by lawyers. He killed Spotted Tail, another Brulé Sioux, who by various accounts was both engaged in a tribal leadership dispute with Crow Dog and was accused of taking liberties with Crow Dog's wife. Crow Dog was convicted in traditional Brulé fashion, and his family paid Spotted Tail's family retribution in the form of money, horses, and a blanket.

Crow Dog was then charged with murder in Dakota Territory Court, convicted, and sentenced to hang. He convinced a clerk of the court to let him spend a few last days with his family, during which most non-Indians expected him to flee. When Crow Dog reported for his hanging on the appointed day, surprising everyone, he became a hero, and non-Indians volunteered to take the case to the United States Supreme Court. Crow Dog was set free, and a precedent was set: Indian courts had jurisdiction in cases of crimes by one Indian against another.

During the following years, the agency became a center for educational programs as well as the land allotment meant to assimilate the Teton Dakotas into "mainstream" life. Between 1904 and 1915, about three-quarters of the reservation's land (as defined by boundaries drawn in 1889) were sold following allotment and opened to non-Indians for settlement.

The Rosebud Agency attempted to convince the reservation residents that they could make a living as farmers on their tracts of 80 or 160 acres (32 or 64 hectares). Farming did not do well in the area, which is frequently arid and subject to extreme swings in temperature from season to season. The Indian agents realized that farming was not compatible with the Indians' heritage or the climate, so they began a livestock breeding program early in the century but abandoned it in 1919. For several decades after that, the reservation offered few economic opportunities to its residents, who lived in some of the most impoverished areas in the United States. Despite the impoverishment, some Brulés became well known. One example was Ben Reifel, who served as a representative in the U.S. Congress for ten years during the 1960s.

SEE ALSO:
Crow Dog; General Allotment Act; Ghost Dance Religion; Reifel, Ben; Siouan Nations; South Dakota; Spotted Tail; Wars, Indian.

ROSE, WENDY (1948–)

Born in Richmond, California, in 1948, Wendy Rose (Hopi-Miwok) was raised in Richmond and Oakland as a Catholic. Separated from her Hopi father, she lived with her Anglo-Miwok mother in an urban environment. Her situation is poignant; not accepted as a clan member among the matrilineal Hopi, her Native heritage was rejected by her mother's relatives.

Keenly aware of her estrangement from Native traditions, Rose uses her poetry to examine her own fragmented life and place in society. She claims her own ground in *The Halfbreed Chronicles and Other Poems*, pondering her own marginal status and that of other victims of colonization who are not necessarily Native American half-breeds, but who represent "half-breededness."

Wendy Rose has been a published poet and artist for over twenty years and has been nominated twice for the Pulitzer Prize in poetry. Although often dubbed as a "protest poet," having willingly served as a voice for various American Indian movement issues, her work is larger and more enduring than that phrase implies.

Rose studied anthropology at the University of California in Berkeley, and she is currently the coordinator of and an instructor in American Indian studies at Fresno City College. A self-described spy, Rose in some of her later poetry pokes sly fun at the idiocies of academia and condemns the violations of the anthropologists who deal with Native American life and culture.

Wendy Rose's works include *Hopi Roadrunner Dancing* (1974); *Long Division: A Tribal History: Poems* (1976); *Academic Squaw: Reports to the World from the Ivory Tower* (1977); *Aboriginal Tattooing in California* (1979); *Builder Kachina: A Home-Going Cycle* (1979); *Lost Copper: Poems* (1980); *What Happened When the Hopi Hit New York* (1982); *The Halfbreed Chronicles and Other Poems* (1985); *Going to War with All My Relations: New and Selected Poems* (1993); *Bone Dance: New and Selected Poems, 1965–1993* (1994); and *Now Poof She Is Gone: Poetry* (1994).